First World War
and Army of Occupation
War Diary
France, Belgium and Germany

3 CAVALRY DIVISION
Divisional Troops
Royal Army Veterinary Corps
13 Mobile Veterinary Section
4 October 1914 - 30 April 1919

WO95/1149/2

The Naval & Military Press Ltd
www.nmarchive.com
Published in association with The National Archives

Published by

The Naval & Military Press Ltd

Unit 10 Ridgewood Industrial Park,

Uckfield, East Sussex,

TN22 5QE England

Tel: +44 (0) 1825 749494

www.naval-military-press.com

www.nmarchive.com

This diary has been reprinted in facsimile from the original. Any imperfections are inevitably reproduced and the quality may fall short of modern type and cartographic standards.

© Crown Copyright
Images reproduced by permission of The National Archives, London, England, 2015.

Contents

Document type	Place/Title	Date From	Date To
Heading	WO95/1149/2		
Heading	3rd Cavalry Division 13th Mobile Vety Section Oct 1914-Apl 1919		
Heading	War Diary of 13th Mobile Vet Section 3rd Cavalry Division October 1914-December-1914		
Heading	War Diary of 13th Mobile Veterinary Section. From 4 Oct. Vol I 1914 To 28 Feb.15		
War Diary	Woolwich	04/10/1914	04/10/1914
War Diary	Southampton	05/10/1914	07/10/1914
War Diary	Ostend	08/10/1914	09/10/1914
War Diary	Bruges	10/10/1914	10/10/1914
War Diary	Thorout	11/10/1914	12/10/1914
War Diary	Roulers	12/10/1914	13/10/1914
War Diary	Ledeghem	14/10/1914	14/10/1914
War Diary	Wytschaete	14/10/1914	16/10/1914
War Diary	Ypres	16/10/1914	16/10/1914
War Diary	Zonnebeke	17/10/1914	18/10/1914
War Diary	Paschendaele	19/10/1914	19/10/1914
War Diary	Poel Capelle	20/10/1914	21/10/1914
War Diary	Zanvoorde	22/10/1914	22/10/1914
War Diary	Zillibeke	23/10/1914	23/10/1914
War Diary	Klein Zillebeke	24/10/1914	26/10/1914
War Diary	Zwarteleen	26/10/1914	27/10/1914
War Diary	Klein Zillebeke	27/10/1914	29/10/1914
War Diary	Zillebeke	30/10/1914	31/10/1914
War Diary	Chateau Ypres	31/10/1914	02/11/1914
War Diary	Hooge	03/11/1914	03/11/1914
War Diary	Farm between Hooge & Halte.	04/11/1914	07/11/1914
War Diary	Halte.	08/11/1914	14/11/1914
War Diary	Nr Vlamertinghe	15/11/1914	20/11/1914
War Diary	Nr Metren	21/11/1914	21/11/1914
War Diary	Merville	22/11/1914	14/12/1914
War Diary	Hondeghem	15/12/1914	15/12/1914
War Diary	Bailleul	16/12/1914	16/12/1914
War Diary	Merville	17/12/1914	30/12/1914
Heading	13th Mobile Vet. Section. 3rd Cavalry Division January-December-1915		
Heading	13th Mobile Vet. Section Jan Feb 1915		
War Diary	Merville	01/01/1915	04/01/1915
War Diary	La Motte-Au-Bois	05/01/1915	06/01/1915
War Diary	Merville	08/01/1915	29/01/1915
War Diary	Thiennes	01/02/1915	04/02/1915
War Diary	Morbecque	05/02/1915	28/02/1915
Heading	War Diary of 13th Mobile Veterinary Section. 3rd Cavalry Division From 1st Mar.1915 To 31st Mar.1915 Vol II		
War Diary	Morbecque.	01/03/1915	31/03/1915
Heading	War Diary of the 13th Mobile Veterinary Section. 3rd Cavalry Division From 1st April 15 To 30th April 15 Vol III		

Miscellaneous	Double Cyanide		
War Diary	Morbecque	01/04/1915	30/04/1915
Heading	3rd Cavalry Division War Diary 13 Mobile Vety Section. 1st May 15 To 31st May 15 Vol IV		
War Diary	Morbecque.	01/05/1915	31/05/1915
Heading	3rd Cavalry Division War Diary 13 Mobile Vety Section. 1st June 15 To 30th June 15 Vol V		
War Diary	Morbecque	01/06/1915	30/06/1915
Heading	3rd Cavalry Division War Diary No.13 Mobile Vety Section. 1July 1915. To 31st July 15. Vol VI		
Heading	13th M. V. S.		
War Diary		01/07/1915	31/07/1915
Heading	3rd Cavalry Division 13th Mobile Vety Section Vol VII August 15		
Heading	War Diary 13th Mobile Vety. Section 1 Aug 1915 To 31st Aug. 1915		
War Diary	Morbecque	01/08/1915	06/08/1915
War Diary	Ligny Lez Aire	07/08/1915	31/08/1915
Heading	3rd Cavalry Division War Diary 13th Mobile Vety Section. 1 Sept. 1915 To 30 Sept 1915 Vol VIII		
War Diary	Ligny Lez Aire	01/09/1915	20/09/1915
War Diary	Bois De Dames	21/09/1915	21/09/1915
War Diary	Ligny Lez Aire	21/09/1915	21/09/1915
War Diary	Bois De Dames	22/09/1915	22/09/1915
War Diary	Westrehem	22/09/1915	22/09/1915
War Diary	Bois De Dames	23/09/1915	23/09/1915
War Diary	Bois des Dams	23/09/1915	23/09/1915
War Diary	Bois De Dames	24/09/1915	24/09/1915
War Diary	Westrehem	24/09/1915	24/09/1915
War Diary	Bois De Dames	25/09/1915	25/09/1915
War Diary	Westrehem	25/09/1915	26/09/1915
War Diary	Rinques	26/09/1915	26/09/1915
War Diary	Nourt Les Mines	27/09/1915	27/09/1915
War Diary	Rinques	27/09/1915	27/09/1915
War Diary	Noeux Les Mines	28/09/1915	28/09/1915
War Diary	Rinques	28/09/1915	28/09/1915
War Diary	Noeux Les Mines	29/09/1915	29/09/1915
War Diary	Rinques.	29/09/1915	29/09/1915
War Diary	Noeux Les Mines	30/09/1915	30/09/1915
War Diary	Rinques	30/09/1915	30/09/1915
Heading	3rd Cavalry Division War Diary 13th Mobile Vety Section. 1Oct.1915. To 31Oct.1915. Vol IX		
War Diary	Bruay.	01/10/1915	01/10/1915
War Diary	Rinques.	01/10/1915	01/10/1915
War Diary	Bruay	02/10/1915	02/10/1915
War Diary	Rinques.	02/10/1915	02/10/1915
War Diary	Bruay	03/10/1915	03/10/1915
War Diary	Rinques.	03/10/1915	03/10/1915
War Diary	Ferfay.	04/10/1915	04/10/1915
War Diary	Rinques.	04/10/1915	04/10/1915
War Diary	Ferfay	05/10/1915	05/10/1915
War Diary	Rinques	05/10/1915	05/10/1915
War Diary	Ferfay	06/10/1915	18/10/1915
War Diary	Palfart	19/10/1915	26/10/1915
War Diary	Auchy-au-Bois	27/10/1915	31/10/1915

Heading	3rd Cavalry Division War Diary No.13 Mobile Vety. Section. From 1st Nov. 15 To 30th Nov 15. Vol X		
War Diary	Auchy au Bois.	01/11/1915	17/11/1915
War Diary	Offin	18/11/1915	21/11/1915
War Diary	Petit Beaurainville	22/11/1915	30/11/1915
Heading	War Diary of No. 13 Mobile Vety. Section From 1st December 1915 To 31st December 1915 Vol XI		
War Diary	Petit Beaurainville	01/12/1915	29/02/1916
War Diary	Lebiez	29/02/1916	15/05/1916
War Diary	Dompierre	15/05/1916	15/05/1916
War Diary	St Riquier	15/05/1916	21/05/1916
War Diary	Le Boisle	21/05/1916	21/05/1916
War Diary	Cavron-St. Martin	21/05/1916	21/05/1916
War Diary	Lebiez	21/05/1916	24/06/1916
War Diary	Domvast	25/06/1916	26/06/1916
War Diary	St. Leger Les-Domart.	26/06/1916	29/06/1916
War Diary	Bonnay	30/06/1916	04/07/1916
War Diary	Merelessart	05/07/1916	08/07/1916
War Diary	Corbie	09/07/1916	09/07/1916
War Diary	Vaux	10/07/1916	19/07/1916
War Diary	La Neuville	20/07/1916	07/08/1916
War Diary	Lebiez	07/08/1916	12/09/1916
War Diary	La Chaussee Tirancourt	13/09/1916	15/09/1916
War Diary	La Neuville	16/09/1916	17/09/1916
War Diary	Pont Noyelles	18/09/1916	22/09/1916
War Diary	Soves	23/09/1916	23/09/1916
War Diary	Saulchoy	24/09/1916	29/09/1916
War Diary	Cucq	30/09/1916	22/12/1916
War Diary	Hesmond	22/12/1916	04/01/1917
War Diary	Petit Beaurain	05/01/1917	30/01/1917
Heading	War Diary of No 13 Mobile Veterinary Section From 1-2-17 To 28-2-17		
War Diary	Petit Beaurain	01/02/1917	08/03/1917
War Diary	La Paix Faite	20/03/1917	28/03/1917
Heading	War Diary of No. 13 Mobile Vety Section. From April 1st 1917 To April 30th 1917		
War Diary	La Paix Faite	03/04/1917	04/04/1917
War Diary	Bouin	05/04/1917	06/04/1917
War Diary	Vacquerie-Le Boucq	07/04/1917	08/04/1917
War Diary	Gouy-en-Artois	09/04/1917	09/04/1917
War Diary	Arras	10/04/1917	15/04/1917
War Diary	Fosseux	16/04/1917	17/04/1917
War Diary	Maintenay	19/04/1917	11/05/1917
War Diary	Tortefontaine	12/05/1917	12/05/1917
War Diary	Frohen Le Grand	13/05/1917	13/05/1917
War Diary	Havernas	14/05/1917	15/05/1917
War Diary	Bussy-Les-Daours	16/05/1917	16/05/1917
War Diary	Bayon Villers	17/05/1917	19/05/1917
War Diary	Buire	24/05/1917	30/05/1917
Heading	War Diary of No.13. Mobile Vety Section From June 1st 1917 To June 30th 1917		
War Diary	Buire	01/06/1917	30/06/1917
Heading	War Diary of No 13 Mobile Vety Section From 1st July 1917 To 31st July 1917		
War Diary	Buire	03/07/1917	03/07/1917
War Diary	Suzanne	04/07/1917	04/07/1917

War Diary	Heilly	05/07/1917	05/07/1917
War Diary	Orville	06/07/1917	06/07/1917
War Diary	Rebreuviette	07/07/1917	07/07/1917
War Diary	Auchel	12/07/1917	16/07/1917
War Diary	Merville	18/07/1917	18/07/1917
War Diary	Les Puresbecques	21/07/1917	27/07/1917
Heading	War Diary of No.13 Mobile Vety Section From 1st August 1917 To 31st August 1917		
War Diary	Les Puresbecques	02/08/1917	17/10/1917
War Diary	Tangry	19/10/1917	19/10/1917
War Diary	Honval	22/10/1917	23/10/1917
War Diary	Gorenflos	24/10/1917	24/10/1917
War Diary	Cocquerel	29/10/1917	30/10/1917
Heading	War Diary of No.13 Mobile Vety Section From Nov 1st 1917 To Nov 30th 1917		
War Diary	Cocquerel	03/11/1917	30/11/1917
Heading	War Diary of No.13 Mobile Vety Section. From 1-12-17 To 31-12-17		
War Diary	Talmas	01/12/1917	02/12/1917
War Diary	Molliens-Au-Bois	07/12/1917	21/12/1917
War Diary	Cocquerel	23/12/1917	31/01/1918
Heading	War Diary of No.13 Mobile Vety Section From 1-1-18 To 31-1-18		
War Diary	Cocquerel	01/01/1918	28/01/1918
War Diary	Belloy-Sur-Somme	29/01/1918	30/01/1918
War Diary	Tertry	31/01/1918	31/01/1918
Heading	War Diary of No.13. Mobile Vety Section. From 1-2-18 To 28-2-18		
War Diary	Tertry	01/02/1918	28/02/1918
Heading	War Diary of No.13 Mobile Vety Section. From 1-3-18 To 31-3-18		
War Diary	Tertry	01/03/1918	12/03/1918
War Diary	Devise	13/03/1918	21/03/1918
War Diary	Beaumont-En-Biene	22/03/1918	22/03/1918
War Diary	Pontoise	23/03/1918	23/03/1918
War Diary	Carlepont	25/03/1918	25/03/1918
War Diary	Ollencourt	26/03/1918	26/03/1918
War Diary	Choisy	27/03/1918	29/03/1918
War Diary	Airion	30/03/1918	30/03/1918
Heading	War Diary of No.13 Mobile Vety Section From 1-4-18 To 30-4-18		
War Diary		01/04/1918	02/04/1918
War Diary	Blangy Tronville	02/04/1918	02/04/1918
War Diary	Fouilly	03/04/1918	05/04/1918
War Diary	Camon	06/04/1918	11/04/1918
War Diary	Boire-Aux-Bois	12/04/1918	12/04/1918
War Diary	Contiville	13/04/1918	13/04/1918
War Diary	Ferfay	13/04/1918	23/04/1918
War Diary	Fontaine	24/04/1918	24/04/1918
War Diary	Lez-Hermanz	24/04/1918	30/04/1918
Heading	War Diary No.13 Mobile Vety Section From 1-5-18 To 31-5-18		
War Diary	Fontaine-Lez-Hermans	02/05/1918	06/05/1918
War Diary	Contay	07/05/1918	17/05/1918
War Diary	Belloy-Sur-Somme	19/05/1918	31/05/1918

Heading	War Diary of No.13 Mobile Vety Section From 1-6-18 To 30-6-18		
War Diary	Montigny	03/06/1918	14/06/1918
War Diary	Belloy Sur-Somme	15/06/1918	16/06/1918
War Diary	Belloy	17/06/1918	29/06/1918
Heading	War Diary of No.13 Mobile Vety Section. From 1-7-18 To 31-7-18		
War Diary	Le-Mesge	01/07/1918	29/07/1918
Heading	War Diary of No.13 Mobile Vety Section. From 1-8-18 To 31-8-18		
War Diary	Le-Mesge	01/08/1918	06/08/1918
War Diary	Renancourt	07/08/1918	07/08/1918
War Diary	Saleux	08/08/1918	13/08/1918
War Diary	Fouencamps	14/08/1918	15/08/1918
War Diary	Le-Mesge	16/08/1918	21/08/1918
War Diary	Fieffes	22/08/1918	26/08/1918
War Diary	Nuncq	27/08/1918	29/08/1918
Heading	War Diary No.13 Mobile Vety Section From 1-9-18 To 30-9-18		
War Diary	Nuncq	01/09/1918	16/09/1918
War Diary	Le-Placiton	19/09/1918	29/09/1918
War Diary	Vermand	30/09/1918	30/09/1918
Heading	War Diary No.13 Mobile Veterinary. Section From 1-10-18 To 31-10-18		
War Diary	Vermand	01/10/1918	05/10/1918
War Diary	Frefcon	06/10/1918	09/10/1918
War Diary	Estrees	09/10/1918	09/10/1918
War Diary	Serain Farm	10/10/1918	14/10/1918
War Diary	Henois Wood	15/10/1918	30/10/1918
Heading	War Diary No.13 Mobile Vety Section. From 1-11-18 To 30-11-18		
War Diary	Hennois Wood	01/11/1918	01/11/1918
War Diary	Manancourt	03/11/1918	15/11/1918
War Diary	Pontenche	16/11/1918	29/11/1918
Heading	War Diary of No.13 Mobile Vety Section From 1-12-18 To 31-12-18		
War Diary	Upigny	03/12/1918	30/12/1918
Heading	War Diary 13 M V S January 1919		
War Diary	Stockay St George Liege 1/100000	01/01/1919	28/02/1919
War Diary	Amay	01/03/1919	22/04/1919
War Diary	Engis	24/04/1919	24/04/1919
War Diary	Amay	23/04/1919	23/04/1919
War Diary	Engis	25/04/1919	30/04/1919

WO 95/1149/2

1914-1919
3RD CAVALRY DIVISION

13TH MOBILE VETY SECTION
OCT 1914 - APL 1919

WAR DIARY

OF

13th MOBILE VET SECTION

3rd CAVALRY DIVISION

OCTOBER 1914 — DECEMBER 1914

Apl 1919

3C

AVD
121/4611

No. 28 Feb. '15.

Confidential.

War Diary

of

13th Mobile Veterinary Section.

Vol I.

From 4 Oct. 1914

Army Form C. 2118.

WAR DIARY
or
INTELLIGENCE SUMMARY.
(Erase heading not required.)

Instructions regarding War Diaries and Intelligence Summaries are contained in F.S. Regs., Part II. and the Staff Manual respectively. Title pages will be prepared in manuscript.

Hour, Date, Place	Summary of Events and Information	Remarks and references to Appendices
4 Oct. '14. WOOLWICH.	Left for Southampton & arrived about 4.30 p.m. proceeded to Rest Camp. JRP	
5 Oct. '14. SOUTHAMPTON	Drew horses at Railway Station for both Sections, 13 + 14, i.e. 30 horses, fitted up harness &c. JRP	
6 Oct. '14. do.	A.S.C. Officer bought two horses for the two Sections, as these were no forage carts with had. JRP	
1.30 p.m. do. do.	Left Rest Camp under orders from DAQMG to proceed to No 2 gate, Southampton Docks, in company with No 14 Section, Major Stone, F.O. ordered us to embark on S.S. MINNESOTA, 2 Officers, 24 N.C.Os & men, 30 horses, 2 lorries. JRP Sailed. JRP	
4. a.m. 7 Oct. '14. do	Arrived & disembarked, spent night on Racecourse JRP	
3.45 p.m. 8 Oct 14 OSTEND.	Left for BRUGES where we arrived at 9.p.m. & billeted in a Nunnery.	
1.30 p.m. 9 Oct '14. do.	9.30 Wilson & Saunders were sent to OSTEND in charge of 16 horses from 1st Royals, also their own two. Sent two 1st Royals transport horses back from STEENE to be treated by Saunders & Wilson JRP	
8. a.m. 10 Oct '14. BRUGES.	Left for LOPHEM & arrived 4 p.m., left again 4.45 p.m. & arrived at THOROUT at 8.p.m. where we billeted. JRP	

WAR DIARY
or
INTELLIGENCE SUMMARY.

(Erase heading not required.)

Army Form C. 2118.

Instructions regarding War Diaries and Intelligence Summaries are contained in F.S. Regs., Part II. and the Staff Manual respectively. Title pages will be prepared in manuscript.

Hour, Date, Place	Summary of Events and Information	Remarks and references to Appendices
10 a.m. 11 Oct 14, THOROUT.	Received our ist maps.	
11 a.m. do. do.	Received 5 horses from 1st Royals which were kept with Section.	
4.15 p.m. do. do.	Drove two horses from H.Q.n	
4.20 p.m. do. do.	Destroyed horse from 1st Royals, suffering from pneumonia & sent to Kneuken.	
5.0 " do. do.	Billets & horses at Hotel St Joseph, Grange St. THOROUT.	
6.45 " do. do.	Was informed of the formation of a Belg. Hospital at BRUGES. Arranged for some lorries at Railway Station to convey horses & Hospitals & advised Capt. Heenan by wire. JRE	
7.25 a.m. 12 Oct 14. do.	Collected 9 Sick Horses from I Hussars, 67 which were put on train to BRUGES, the 7b being too exhausted was conveyed on a lorry to Hotel St Joseph, Grange St. THOROUT. Your horses left at the Hotel on day previous was also put on train for BRUGES, as was chargent. St Stokes I Hussars. A chestnut transport horse belonging to R[?]d Hd'qrs was left at Hotel St Joseph, having been given ovasdine gr. 17, it was considered undesirable to risk the train journey which it was suffering from laminitis. A horse St. K R.H.A. was put on train to BRUGES.	
10.15 a.m. do. do.	Sick ent from THOROUT to BRUGES. 12. Left at Hotel St Joseph. 2.	

WAR DIARY
~~INTELLIGENCE~~ SUMMARY.
(Erase heading not required.)

Army Form C. 2118.

Instructions regarding War Diaries and Intelligence Summaries are contained in F.S. Regs., Part II. and the Staff Manual respectively. Title pages will be prepared in manuscript.

Hour, Date, Place		Summary of Events and Information	Remarks and references to Appendices
10.15 a.m.	12 Oct '14 THOROUT	Left for ROULERS.	
2.25 p.m.	do. ROULERS	Arrived + at 2.40 pm received a horse from 15th Bde. Ammunition Col.	
3.25 p.m.	do. do.	Received message from A.D.V.S. notifying removal of Horse Vety Hospital from BRUGES to DUNKIRK. Received orders from B/de Major, 6th Cav. Bde. to have Reveille 4.30 a.m. Horses harnessed + Breakfast 5 a.m. Officers Breakfast 5.30 a.m. wagon to be packed + loaded down JRP.	
	13 Oct 14 do.	Ariped 4 horses to Dunkirk, H/Q samples in charge + certificate etc Raw Hospital.	
10.4 m.	do. do.	Started for LEDEGHEM + arrived 11 p.m. JRP.	
	14 Oct 14 LEDEGHEM	Left 3 horses with Burgomaster who promised to entrain them + recollegt of Horse Vety Hospital, DUNKIRK.	
5.45 a.m.	do. do.	Left for WYTSCHAETE	
10 p.m.	do. WYTSCHAETE	Arrived + Billets. JRP	
	15 Oct 14 do.	Took over 50 horses + kept them with Section - remained here all day. JRP	
	16 · 14 do.	Took over one horse from 6th Cav. Bde. Hd. Qu. V, left at 7.30 a.m. Will of side horse for ZONNEBEKE. Lt Cooper's horse dropped from exhaustion about 2 miles from YPRES, got horse up + had him at Cooper rode on wagon.	

WAR DIARY
or
INTELLIGENCE SUMMARY.
(Erase heading not required.)

Army Form C. 2118.

Instructions regarding War Diaries and Intelligence Summaries are contained in F.S. Regs., Part II. and the Staff Manual respectively. Title pages will be prepared in manuscript.

Hour, Date, Place	Summary of Events and Information	Remarks and references to Appendices
16.10.14. YPRES	Boyd & Horan but was unable to notify the Base City Hospital as all communications were cut from DUNKIRK & BOULOGNE. Delayed 2 hours at ST JULIEN. Major Berry being here, arrived at ZONNEBEKE at 9 p.m. & billeted. J.R.B.	
5 a.m. 17 Oct/14 ZONNEBEKE	Took over two horses from 1st Royals, one he bought was left behind in charge of L. Vandervyver, at St Jappe ton. ZONNEBEKE. who signed a receipt for it & agreed to feed & water it until called for. Genl. Hakins charger was treated for a wound, hide on stifle. Took over 3 more horses from 1st Royals & treated them, also another from 6th Cav: Bde. Mid. Dns. remained all day at ZONNEBEKE. Took over Lord Naions charger, one from 1st Royals & one from 16th Rbr. Ammunition Col. Started at 12.30 pm, with the 10 horses taken over & arrived at YPRES at 2 p.m. kept the 10 horses here for DUNKIRK having notified the O/C. Base City Hospital by wire from ZONNEBEKE before starting, returned to ZONNEBEKE at 4.30 p.m.	J.R.B.
18. Oct.14. do.	Started from here immediately for PASSCHENDAELE. Arrived here about 6.30 p.m. & billeted for night.	

WAR DIARY or INTELLIGENCE SUMMARY

Army Form C. 2118.

(Erase heading not required.)

Instructions regarding War Diaries and Intelligence Summaries are contained in F.S. Regs., Part II. and the Staff Manual respectively. Title pages will be prepared in manuscript.

Hour, Date, Place	Summary of Events and Information	Remarks and references to Appendices
18-10-14	On my return for ZONNEBEKE I was informed that A.M.S had used K Railway Station at YPRES, nothing however to be forwarded to BOULOGNE. Also that Major Chamberlain A.S.C. had gone sick & was taken sick by R.A.M.C. JRE	
6 a.m. 19-10-14 PASSCHENDAELE	Left & concentrated at Railway Station, two of my men went to the trenches, the others held horses for armd men, retired to POEL CAPELLE 7 arrived at 7.30 p.m. at Alltkids. JRE	
6.10 a.m. 20-10-14. POEL CAPELLE	Took our three horses from 1st Royals, shot one of them, very lame, supporting sick, brought other two out to St JULIEN & thence to a spot between ST JULIEN & LANGEMARCK, where we stopped the night on the road side. JRE	
H.Q.m. 21-10-14.	Proceeded on way & arrived at YPRES at 7.30 a.m. took over 5 horses from 1st Royals & 2 from II Hussars. which were logged at YPRES with the two taken over yesterday. O/C B.V. Hospital was informed as was D.D.V.S. G.H.Q. left about 8.20 a.m. & arrived at HOOGE & took over 3 more horses from 1st Royals & one from 2nd Lp Gds. which I sent back to YPRES + Mr Sudow took them over, pending their despatch to HAVRE at a later hour, & also informed c/o B.V. Hospital & D.D.V.S. started for ZANVOORDE & arrived about 12.30 p.m. stayed the night, village was deserted. JRE	

WAR DIARY
or
INTELLIGENCE SUMMARY.
(Erase heading not required.)

Army Form C. 2118.

Instructions regarding War Diaries and Intelligence Summaries are contained in F.S. Regs., Part II. and the Staff Manual respectively. Title pages will be prepared in manuscript.

Hour, Date, Place	Summary of Events and Information	Remarks and references to Appendices
7.30 a.m. 22-10-14. ZANVOORDE	Left for Zillebeke which we left again at about 9.30 a.m. & went to YPRES where took over 2 horses from 1st Royals, who both E. a German horse, both suffering from Debility & weakness. Later took over another horse from 1st Royals. brought on there 3 horses with Section to ZILLEBEKE as there was no time to bed them. Arrived at ZILLEBEKE about 7.30 p.m. & picketed in a field here for the night. JRP	
23.10.14. ZILLEBEKE.	Received two horses from C Batt. R.H.A. 1 Kick other & 1 necrosis if of Pastern, latter destroyed & buried. 1st Royals (C19's Germany) both girth galls, & C Dy Fusiliers wither & C 311. Started at 4.50 a.m for YPRES with these three horses + the 3 received overnight + Type the Lt for ROUEN, informed O/C ROUEN by wire & also DDVS for Major Barry, arrived back at ZILLEBEKE at 10.45 a.m & started for KLEIN ZILLEBEKE about 11.30 a.m, having taken over horses from 2nd Life Guards & another Transport horse, took & picketed we brought with us. Receives note from A.D.V.S to retain Sick horses with Unit. JRP.	
7.a.m. 24.10.15. KLEIN ZILLEBEKE	Left & went back with Transport as far as YPRES, whilst Rice took on two horses from RE's which were unable to be moved. These	

WAR DIARY
or
INTELLIGENCE SUMMARY
(Erase heading not required.)

Army Form C. 2118.

Instructions regarding War Diaries and Intelligence Summaries are contained in F.S. Regs., Part II. and the Staff Manual respectively. Title pages will be prepared in manuscript.

Hour, Date, Place	Summary of Events and Information	Remarks and references to Appendices
	were left in charge of Eugene Biddleson, 43 Hondstraat, YPRES. Forage being provided by me. Joined Brigade Transport just outside YPRES & went on to KLEIN ZILLEBEKE for the night. JRB	
7.30 a.m. 25.10.14. KLEIN ZILLEBEKE	left & went with transport as far as YPRES road. Met A.D.V.S. + was informed that all sick horses were to be sent to Base Vet: Hospital, ABBEVILLE. Took over 3 horses at ZWARTEDEEN (1 Z Hussar + 2 R.H.A.) There were brought along with the two taken on the 23 out of ZILLEBEKE & 5 more were taken from 1st Notts. Section at ZILLEBEKE near CHEMIN "Lower 32 hours from Z Hussar & one from C Batt R.H.A. R--- Base at YPRES went to HONDSTRAAT as for the two horses left yesterday, one had died this morning but the other & the Station & found that the French wounded had occupied all the horse boxes so left horses at the Ecole d'Equitation & reported to 2nd 6th Cav. R-- at 9 P.M. & went back to CHEMIN with transport. JRB	
26.10.14. NEAR KLEIN ZILLEBEKE	Took 14 horses down to YPRES (9 were 11th Hussars, 4 -1st RD, 1 C Batt R.H.A.) There were hopes that somebody's 3rd Scale of Equitation stated our the 55 left with 11th London yesterday, one of these was in a very bad state so was taken back & shot. Capt Heavens was trying	

WAR DIARY or INTELLIGENCE SUMMARY

Army Form C. 2118.

Instructions regarding War Diaries and Intelligence Summaries are contained in F.S. Regs., Part II. and the Staff Manual respectively. Title pages will be prepared in manuscript.

(Erase heading not required.)

Hour, Date, Place	Summary of Events and Information	Remarks and references to Appendices
26.10.14 ZWARTELEEN	Horses &c took over from S whit & had given one yesterday. Were leaving one with 43 b bat. o/c D.D.V.S. G.H.Q. on behalf of Major Barry. Received letter telegram at ZWARTELEEN. Continue to night. JRB	
27.10.14 do.	Took over 3 horses from 18 Hussars, 2 from C.O.D of T.R.H.A, 1 from L/C B N° 2. One from F(Bat T.R.H.A. These were brought to YPRES & kept except 1 from I Hussars which died at ZILLEBEKE. Continue for night. JRB	
28.10.14 KLEIN ZILLEBEKE		
29.10.14 " "	Roped 11 horses at YPRES. 9 — 1st Dragoons & 2 18th Hussars. D.D.V.S. made & railed horses unable to walk to be sent to JRB	
29.10.14 " "	Visited 18 Hussars & got A.F.B 2010 which I handed to A.D.V.S. also one for my own Unit. JRB	
30.10.14 ZILLEBEKE	Went with transport to YPRES & took over 3 horses from 18 Hussars also one from 4th Field Ambulance. These were taken at YPRES to Abbeville. JRB	
31.10.14 do.	Went to YPRES with transport & took 2 horses from 1st Royals, 1 Police &c & one found on road. 3 R.E's & General Stoken's Charger. These were bought to Railway & sent to Abbeville.	

WAR DIARY
or
INTELLIGENCE SUMMARY.
(Erase heading not required.)

Army Form C. 2118.

Hour, Date, Place	Summary of Events and Information	Remarks and references to Appendices
31.10.14. CHATEAU YPRES.	Bivouac for night in garden. JRB	
1-11-14. " "	Blamyel Section with Transport to HOOGE, took over 6 horses from I Hussars brought them to YPRES, left them at Ecole d'Equitation as there were no trucks. JRB	
2.11.14. " "	Bivouac for night in garden. Left with Transport & arrived at HALT, took over horses from I Hussars, was wounded N E.44 to 5 to tie in the head, 2 from 6th Field Amb. Also from 3rd R.E. there were horses together all 5 of the 6 horses taken from I Hussars yesterday (the other was taken over by my section to Zantvoort). Pack stallion charger was also badly making a total of 12. Bastinges 3 horses badly wounded at HALT. JRB	
3-11-14. HOOGE.	Bivouac in garden at HOOGE for night. JRB Took 2 horses from I Hussars, 1 from 1st Royals, 1 Belgian found on road, no horses my own section, all wounded. Led it to him at YPRES but found that no trains were running. So took him on to Cold. Stream at VLAMERTINGHE. He knew from I Hussars and no earlier on memory with wound in chest was destroyed by XII Section at YPRES. All HOGE who section are to later our day	

Forms/C. 2118/10

WAR DIARY
or
INTELLIGENCE SUMMARY.
(Erase heading not required.)

Army Form C. 2118.

Hour, Date, Place	Summary of Events and Information	Remarks and references to Appendices
4-11-14. Farm between HOOGE & HALTE.	men of XIV Section + to collect from both 1st & 7th Brigades, 3rd Cav Division. When I returned from VLAMERTINGHE I found that four horses had been handed over by Major Pellin, R.H.G. also their Cart in by A.D.V.S. These were brought in by Section to a farm midway between HOOGE & HALTE. Bivouac at this farm for night. JRR	
5-11-14. do.	Took over horse from C Bty RHA & sent it with R.7 taken last evening & Capt Neame, with I Fromow, R.H.G, 1st Royals taken over 4 day. Capt Neame kept the 6 men who had been sent to me yesterday. JRR Took over 2 horses from B Sect. 6 S.Y.Q. V. went with Rees myself to see Capt Neame about the 6 men detained yesterday & he moved me to proceed to POPERINGHE to buy 55 horses to ABBEVILLE, he having given me a written order. A few of our men from hosp. rd. during the night. There were no casualties in our Section. JRR	
6-11-14 do.	Sent F.F.R. 2010 to A.D.V.S & A.F.D. 213 to R.G.s Officer R.H. Bde. JRR Took over 2 horses from 3rd Dragoons.	
7-11-14 do.	Took over 1 horse to C Batt R.H.A. + 1 from 3rd D.Gs and three two with horses taken from 3rd Dragoons yesterday, also a lame front	

WAR DIARY
or
INTELLIGENCE SUMMARY

(Erase heading not required.)

Army Form C. 2118.

Instructions regarding War Diaries and Intelligence Summaries are contained in F. S. Regs., Part II. and the Staff Manual respectively. Title pages will be prepared in manuscript.

Hour, Date, Place	Summary of Events and Information	Remarks and references to Appendices
8-11-14 HAZE E.	in neighbourhood. Unit unknown. Received 7 p.m. O.O. No. 114/75. There 5 were taken over by Capt Heaven. He Russell was given a horse in exchange for his own. Crowd with transport at St JERN took over those transport horses from I Division. Brooke for night at HAZE JRB. Heaved over to Capt Heaven the 3 transport horses from I Division I received and to replace one sick of my own addition. Bivouacked here for night. JRB	
9-11-14. do	Took own 3 horses from I Division. Change to POPERINGHE. When I was ordered to take 104 horses led still on the good road ahead to them at BAILLEUL. Started 32, got orders from Capt Rawlis asking that it was with the 22 horses. At D.N.S. in BAILLEUL, he gave us instructions as to the Sergeant but own 5 horses from 2nd Dragoons at HALTE of which one will Rawlins. died during night. JRB	
10-11-14 do	Stayed at BAILLEUL with the 4 with own horse & some of the sick or Remainder of sick horses and the 4 to horse from 3rd Dragoons a Capt Heaven, whilst I at BAILLEUL loops 7 horses in	

Capt Heaven

WAR DIARY
or
INTELLIGENCE SUMMARY
(Erase heading not required.)

Army Form C. 2118.

Instructions regarding War Diaries and Intelligence Summaries are contained in F. S. Regs., Part II. and the Staff Manual respectively. Title pages will be prepared in manuscript.

Hour, Date, Place	Summary of Events and Information	Remarks and references to Appendices
11-11-14 HALTE.	A waggon & cart of wine ABEEVILLE with Rum, two horses, waiting. Pte 104 had to be destroyed at TRILLEUL JRE. Went over & drew from 3rd Dragoons 4 sets Rein & Capt Hearne 4 Capts., also took over 1 transport line from X Hussars + 6 from 1st Royals. Took Rein to Capt Hearne + was given Hothin to Col at POPERINGHE, who I asked this Railway was about to having to brought them back & returned to HALTE. JRE	
12-11-14 "	Went over 2 horses from C Bty R.H.A. + 1 from X Hussars JRE	
13-11-14 "	" " 1 " " K. " + handed them 3 over to Capt Hearne. Maj Callin aust some horses to Capt Hearne. Arrived one R Arc R.H.A. Leave. O.F. unable to ——— do 2 Lts + JRE.	
14-11-14 "	Took over 5 horses from X Hussars, 6 from 3rd Dragoons, 1 unknown & handed them over to Capt Hearne. JRE	
15-11-14 Nr VLAMERTINGHE	1 - 3rd Dragoons horses knocked + Capt Hearne took over 20 horses wounded from 1st Brigade + 4 myself threw at POPERINGHE. JRE	
16-11-15 do.	Took over 22 wounded horses from 1st Royals + 4 from X Hussars + buried them at POPERINGHE. JRE	

WAR DIARY
INTELLIGENCE SUMMARY
(Erase heading not required.)

Army Form C. 2118.

Hour, Date, Place	Summary of Events and Information	Remarks and references to Appendices
17-11-14 Jn VLAMERTINGHE	Took over 3 horses from 5th Dragoons. JRB	
18-11-14 do.	" " " " 8 " " C Bat. R.H.A. JRB	
19-11-14 do.	Boyes following horses at POPERINGHE, 14 q from 1st Section. 21 from 13 Relief. 12 from 1st Royals. Total 87. Shot one we had evacuated.	
20-11-14 do.	Took over 14 horses from X Hussars & 14 from 3rd Dragoons, one of the latter was in such a bad state at Railway Station had to evacuate he would not reach ABBEVILLE alive & shot him. & also took 14 horses from 1st Section. Total 41 horses. Afterwards started for La COURONNE & reached village near METREN where we stayed the night B.JRB	
21-11-14 110 METREN.	Started to LACOURONNE & was ordered to MERVILLE where we arrived at 3:45 pm & took up quarters at a farm near Mh O. it C.Bdr. JRB.	
22-11-14 MERVILLE	Ordered to move to another farm & went to Mme Ypainné Rouban where I took over 6 horses from 3rd Dragoons JRB.	
23-11-14 do.	Took over 2 horses from Sig troop 6th Cav Bde. JRB	
24-11-14 do.	" " " " " HQ " " N Souvrich Germany.	

WAR DIARY or INTELLIGENCE SUMMARY

Army Form C. 2118.

Instructions regarding War Diaries and Intelligence Summaries are contained in F. S. Regs., Part II. and the Staff Manual respectively. Title pages will be prepared in manuscript.

(Erase heading not required.)

Hour, Date, Place	Summary of Events and Information	Remarks and references to Appendices
24-11-14 MERVILLE	Received 4 horses from 1st Regt. & 4 from 8th Dragoons. Regt 48 horses at HAZEBROUCK. Capt Heaven FB. un-blocking about 20 bucket-beat them with my Section. Lt Cooper landed on the air from 3rd Dragoons at Hazebrouck station & informed me he had distemper one had had an open back joint. JRB	
25-11-14	Called at Optincur Stores, Hazebrouck & received 4 horses under vet. orders sent in to. Lt Cooper dropped on 9/16 N.S.Y horses which had been handed over in the 24th, as he had orders to take for any treatment. JRB	
26-11-14	Visited N.S.Y. & made an R.F.A 2000. Inspected saddlery & wrote report under instructions from Brig. Gen. 6th Cav. Bde. JRB	
27-11-14	Took over 3 horses from HQ 2/c Sect 15th Bde, R.H.A. JRB	
28-11-14	" 1 " 1st Royals & one from 3rd Dragoons R. Horse Gn before 21 at HAZEBROUCK	
29-11-14	Visited K.C. & G Btys. ~ Ammunition Col. Took over 1 horse from Capt Atkinson, Sig through H 2" 6th Cav Bde JRB	

WAR DIARY
or
INTELLIGENCE SUMMARY

(Erase heading not required.)

Army Form C. 2118.

Instructions regarding War Diaries and Intelligence Summaries are contained in F. S. Regs., Part II. and the Staff Manual respectively. Title pages will be prepared in manuscript.

Hour, Date, Place	Summary of Events and Information	Remarks and references to Appendices
30-11-14 MERVILLE	Handed over of the N.S.Yeomanry Lines & went to HAZEBROUCK & saw Major Berry. Took over 10 horses from 3rd Dragoons & Capt Smyth from Cavalry Corps. Also 2 from Transport 3 Cav Div. Major Zuchini asked for a return of sick horses in Units of 6 Cav Bde taken over by my section from 24th exchange with Division on termination what was given has arrived. JRB	
1-12-14 "	Inspected sick of N.S.Y. & went to HAZEBROUCK & kept appointment with Major Berry at H.Q.C.B. his clerk however informed me that he was in (pretty) unit's [illeg] inspect my section at 2.0.Clk. Major Berry inquired at time stated & gave me returns for R.H.A. (K.C.G. (Btie)) & Armoured Cl. N.S.Yeomanry sung own with & the number from 6 C.G. up to present. Also inspectles 15 horses from Kemps & Base Vety hospital. Returned on horse N.S.Yeomanry to duty. Visited Brig. Genl Campbells charges freehes O.F. JRB Martin N.S.Yeomanry Brig. Genl charges, Capt Depree at J.O Clk. Shot one horse of 3rd Dragoons	
2-12-14 "		

WAR DIARY
or
INTELLIGENCE SUMMARY
(Erase heading not required.)

Army Form C. 2118.

Hour, Date, Place		Summary of Events and Information	Remarks and references to Appendices
3-12-14	MERVILLE	Started for HAZEBROUCK with 15 horses + took them also another horse A.S.C. 2 Cav. Res. where the RTO asked me to send with my R.t. Got transport 1,000 for farm Cashel 2nd Cav. Bre. for men's pay & transport for forage when necessary. Visited C + G Bties. + Ammunition Col. 15th Bde. R.H.A. + called at JRB	
4-12-14	do	Returned 2 horses to 3rd D.G. one of which was returned. K Bty. for their return prich, also at LC of 2, 15th Bde. + N.S/oon. Visited R.W. Artillery + Ammunition Col. also N.S/oon. + went to HAZEBROUCK making out return with Capt. Stevens. JRB	
5-12-14	do	Visited K + C Bties. + Ammunition Col. + Horse to HAZEBROUCK with returns. Saw Serj. of Yeomanry. JRB	
6-12-14	do	Called at N.S.Y. men to HAZEBROUCK, finished returns walked at Opheme to Meganu + my wish wagon turned it & got it repairs locally + pair for it & money being afterwards refunded by O.C. Admitted one horse from 1st R.D's two from 3rd D.G. Discharged two cures to 1st R. Royals, 1 to R. 2nd Cavalry Depo + three to 3rd Dragoons. JRB	

WAR DIARY or INTELLIGENCE SUMMARY

Army Form C. 2118.

(Erase heading not required.)

Instructions regarding War Diaries and Intelligence Summaries are contained in F. S. Regs., Part II. and the Staff Manual respectively. Title pages will be prepared in manuscript.

Hour, Date, Place	Summary of Events and Information	Remarks and references to Appendices
7-12-14. MERVILLE.	Billeted 31 Horses at MERVILLE. JRB	
8-12-14 "	Visited N.S. Yorks. C. & K. Battns. & Numnum Co. JRB	
9-12-14 "	Major Barry called for me in morning to go round visits of the B'de with him. JRB	
10-12-14 "	C.O.C. 6th Co. R.B.G. held an inspection of N.S. Yeomanry. I was present as V.O. pro tem & was finished at 1.30 pm. Visited sick of "G" Batt R.H.A. & made out A.F.A. 2090 for 15th & 13th Co. R.H.A. & 4 of 1st Batt relieved returnees from ABBEVILLE referred me & the sick of a horse evacuate to hospital. G.O.C. ordered me to inspect horses of N.S.Y. again to recommend a number fit for duty at present & in a weeks time. JRB	
11-12-14 " 9.15 a.m.	Started for N.S.Y. & inspected all the sick horses seen yesterday & forwarded a report to Brig. Gen 6th Cav.Bde. by his orders. Inspected & treated those of H+C Sqdns. & some of B. Sqdn. which I was unable to finish as it was dark. Sick in. 17 cases sent by A.D.V.S. from R. Har. Co, Mtd Div at 10a.m. Sent Lt Colpun with me as I was engaged as above. JRB	

WAR DIARY
or
INTELLIGENCE SUMMARY

(Erase heading not required.)

Army Form C. 2118.

Instructions regarding War Diaries and Intelligence Summaries are contained in F. S. Regs., Part II. and the Staff Manual respectively. Title pages will be prepared in manuscript.

Hour, Date, Place	Summary of Events and Information	Remarks and references to Appendices
12-12-14. MERVILLE. 9.a.m.	Inspected B Sqdn & M.G. Yeom. Proceeded on list to Brig Genl L.J. Capper both in hands of the Para Hospital under instructions from A.D.M.S. which he received yesterday. On his return he informed me that he had received this 5X hours Received an wire from H.A. 2/c 6 Cav. Bde. Hondeg. on my way & the 10th Bde. Ammunition Col. & overseer me from M.S.Yeomanry. The wagon loaded me & me had a list of the O.F. Spring tubes. Went to R.H.A + Ammunition Col. & saw about wagon & took over. JRB	
13-12-14. do.	Horses from 3rd Dragoons, R.H.A. + M.S.Yeomanry. JRB Rode 32 horses at HAZEBROUCK & slept the night HONDEGHEM. JRB	
14-12-14. do.		
15-12-14. HONDEGHEM.	Started at 8.a.m. for BAILLEUL & took up quarters at Avenue de la Gare. JRB	
16-12-14 BAILLEUL.	Took over 11 horses from 3rd Dragoons + 6 from 19 Royals. Horses were inspected by Major Benny at about 12.30 p.m. Rendered over 16 to be destroyed. Roped 16 + sent returning party & started for Merville at 3.0 p.m. arrived at 4.45 p.m. JRB	
17-12-14. MERVILLE.	Visited H.T.C. Sqdn M.S.Yeom. Horses & Carthorses. JRB	

WAR DIARY
or
INTELLIGENCE SUMMARY

Army Form C. 2118.

Hour, Date, Place		Summary of Events and Information	Remarks and references to Appendices
18-12-14	MERVILLE	Sent 25 horses to Base Rly Hospital, Boulogne. JRB	
19-12-14	"	Took over ward at Boulogne the following lines: to Ridge gdn, 6 I Horses, 1 Easy Germ. Stat 17. Have been inspected by Major Pemy of Shipbrook Sta who retained 9 Horses & 2 Easy Germ. JRB	
20-12-14	"	Took two cases from RHA & returned for treatment. Yorked 6th Rgt. Hd. Qrs. & one General Horse & Major Liebie suffering from pneumonia. Reported 2 mange cases in NSY. JRB. Had mange cases dressed with mixture. Took one horse from Boyab. JRB.	
22-12-14	"	Sent two mange cases to ABBEVILLE. 1 RHA horse which I had given no stings. Came back kind of inflection, dice. JRB. Yorks N.S.Veterinary. JRB	
23-12-14	"		
24-12-14	"	I went on 168 hours leave. JRB	
26-12-14	"	Sgt Panupton, forench Interpreter joined Section. JRB	

WAR DIARY

OF

13TH MOBILE VET SECTION.

3RD CAVALRY DIVISION

JANUARY – DECEMBER – 1915

13TH MOBILE VET. SECTION

Jan Feb 1915

WAR DIARY or INTELLIGENCE SUMMARY

Army Form C. 2118.

(Erase heading not required.)

Instructions regarding War Diaries and Intelligence Summaries are contained in F. S. Regs., Part II. and the Staff Manual respectively. Title pages will be prepared in manuscript.

Hour, Date, Place	Summary of Events and Information	Remarks and references to Appendices
1-1-15 MERVILLE.	Returned from leave. 1 Horse taken from N.S.Y. JRP	
2-1-15 "	Sgt Harrison RVC Reports for duty from Vet Section. Unobirigte two horses. 1 from N.S.Y. & 1 from 1st Royals. JRP	
3-1-15 "	1 Mange case taken from N.S.Y. sent to Abbeville. 8 horses sent to Base Vety Shop Steenwerck. Sgt Stonehewer Strefield to formation R Paff Sigt. 15 cases admitted from N.S.Y. JRP	
4-1-15 "	Cpt Grist at Merville to La Motte-au-Bois, had accommodation satisfactory starting for horses & and supply places for men. One horse received from newspaper 2nd Essex Adv. JRP	
5-1-15. LA MOTTE-AU-BOIS	Visited horses at Rue du Bois a address not same from C.C.N.2. Gt Vet sent & inspected, Slimed poisoning. JRP	
6-1-15 "	Returned to hilt by Wm Ypsines Bureau Merville. JRP	
8-1-15 MERVILLE.	One case suspected mange taken from N.S.Y horse sent to Abbeville. Sent over 2 Gruenifort horses from 6th Cav Bde MI 2i/c. JRP	
9 & 10-1-15 "	nil JRP	

WAR DIARY
or
INTELLIGENCE SUMMARY
(Erase heading not required.)

Army Form C. 2118.

Instructions regarding War Diaries and Intelligence Summaries are contained in F. S. Regs., Part II. and the Staff Manual respectively. Title pages will be prepared in manuscript.

Hour, Date, Place	Summary of Events and Information	Remarks and references to Appendices
11-1-15 MERVILLE	Admitted 2 horses from F. Jenson & from Sussex Yeom. & sent them on to NEUFCHATEL. Major Berry inspected before going. JRB.	
12-1-15 "	Detained horse from C.C.H° D° Kelso now on the 5th. Admitted 4 from N.S. Yeom. JRB. Discharged 2 horses cured to N.S.Y. JRB.	
13-1-15 "		
14-1-15 "	Major Berry inspected horses under treatment at billet & ordered 2 detained to die. inspected one suspected strange case from N.S.Y. 1 Capt. 1 Sowr. 4 Burials reported for duty from Neufchatel. JRB.	
15-1-15 "	Visited sick horse at Rue d'Ypres. Capt Goldsmid & D'Owens R.E. about sick a sent to Sick Conv. Horse and neck & sections & Bellemath to Anyfield. Seven horses moved to hospital by Major Berry were sent to-day. the eighth became unable on the road to Strazeleneele Iwas sent back to billet left care of dresser. Lt. Bell R.H.A. at offices g R.D.V.S. JRB. Visited N.S. Yeom. Sherm Barry calls & on section but I did not meet him. Discharged one horse to R. War Leta cured. Capt. Bellewell reports in duty from Hospital. JRB.	
16-1-15 "		

WAR DIARY or INTELLIGENCE SUMMARY

Army Form C. 2118.

Instructions regarding War Diaries and Intelligence Summaries are contained in F. S. Regs., Part II. and the Staff Manual respectively. Title pages will be prepared in manuscript.

(Erase heading not required.)

Hour, Date, Place	Summary of Events and Information	Remarks and references to Appendices
18-1-15 MERVILLE	Visited N.S. Yorks. J.R.B.	
19-1-15 "	Sent to Hazebrouck to take 7 horses, apply received that were required for three days, sent to Merville, were informed that could have from at 1 p.m. tomorrow, asked Major Barry to meet us there to arrange to do so at 10.30 a.m. to-morrow. J.R.B.	
20-1-15 "	Major Barry inspected 11 horses from Pt. Horse Gds. & one from I Dragoons. 10 of the former were ordered to Base Hospital with one from N.S.Y. which require treatment here. (Rept. Th. 11 horse at Merville.) The horses sent with C Coys. 11th & 12th Cavalry were syphon & A.D. Rock did not consider them fit to move to other work. Pt. Lugwell sent to Hospital, with varicose vein & returned to duty. — Pt. Lugwell arrives and to Hospital & returns to duty. — J.R.B. horse arrives from C.C. 1st Div. J.R.B.	
21-1-15 "		
22-1-15 "	One horse received from 1st Royals. " from 1st Div. C.C. Horses moto Guidens horse attacks 1st Div. J.R.B.	
23-1-15 "	Seven 4 horses from B Dragoons. Bishops in horse. 1st D.C.C. (Mental Steinus). J.R.B.	

Army Form C. 2118.

WAR DIARY
or
INTELLIGENCE SUMMARY
(Erase heading not required.)

Instructions regarding War Diaries and Intelligence Summaries are contained in F. S. Regs., Part II. and the Staff Manual respectively. Title pages will be prepared in manuscript.

Hour, Date, Place	Summary of Events and Information	Remarks and references to Appendices
24-1-15 MERVILLE	Received 2 horses I. Hussars. JRP	
25-1-15 "	" 2 " 5th Dragoons	
	" 1 " H.S. 2nd 1st Cav. Bde.	
	13 Sick horses taken to who Peters. Robin Lévêque, Le Sart.	
	Capt Stone left in charge JRP	
26-1-15 "	Received 2 horses from N.S.Y	
	" 8 " " Soan X. JRP	
27-1-15 "	" 2 Remounts from 6th Cav Bde.	
	" 4 " " Cav Corps	
	" 1 Sick horse N.S.Y	
	" 1 " " 3 D.G.	
	" 2 " " R.H.G. Jas. JRP.	
28-1-15 "	2 horse destroyed, one of Remounts to Boulogne 19 ache to Hazebrouck	
29-1-15 "	Changed billet to THIENNES. farm of Mme FLEURY. JRP	
	Visit Capt Glynns charger could'nt move JRP	
1-2-15 THIENNES	Received Emergent horse from 3rd Bde 1st Cav Bde. put down sep os. JRP	

Army Form C. 2118.

WAR DIARY
or
INTELLIGENCE SUMMARY
(Erase heading not required.)

Instructions regarding War Diaries and Intelligence Summaries are contained in F. S. Regs., Part II. and the Staff Manual respectively. Title pages will be prepared in manuscript.

Hour, Date, Place		Summary of Events and Information	Remarks and references to Appendices
2-2-15	THIENNES	Relieved my own charge JRP	
3-2-15	"	Visits N° 20 horses. Received 2 from N.S.Y. S.S. Gourlay transferred to M Section. JRP	
4-2-15	"	Changes billets to M me Cotteatts Carrière, Morbecque. 2 short soldiers from SERCUS. Driver Devereux reports sick. Sent to hospital where he was retained. JRP	
5-2-15	MORBECQUE	Received one horse from N.S.Y. Sh. Loops attended Hospital & Reg't. injured knees. discuss JRP	
6-2-15	"	Proceed 2 horses from 1 Regt. Buckingham horse from N° 2 transport. stiff joint. JRP	
7-2-15	"	Major Berry collect & inspects WAR. Pte Rhonsfield reports from N° 2 Section Hospital. Recover JRP	
8-2-15	"	Two horses received from I Lancers. Mad return from Major Berry of F.D.V.S. Cavalry Corps JRP	
9-2-15	"	Major Berry calls with D.D.V.S. + Colonel S! Renoaults JRP	
10-2-15	"	One horse from N.S.Y. discharged cust to 3 rd Dragoons JRP	
11-2-15	"	8 horses sent to Base Vet'y Hospital. JRP.	

WAR DIARY
or
INTELLIGENCE SUMMARY

(Erase heading not required.)

Army Form C. 2118.

Instructions regarding War Diaries and Intelligence Summaries are contained in F. S. Regs., Part II. and the Staff Manual respectively. Title pages will be prepared in manuscript.

Hour, Date, Place		Summary of Events and Information	Remarks and references to Appendices
12-2-15	MORBECQUE	36 Mange cases brought in by N.S.Y. & sent back until fit returns by Major Barry JRB	
13-2-15	"	34 Mange cases from N.S.Y sent to Steenbecque. 2 horses received from 1st Royals JRB	
14-2-15	"	Two mange cases received from N.S.Y. Met Major Barry + Hunter at rail Station Hellet JRB	
15-2-15	"	Received 3 susp. mange cases from B " Dragoons. 9 ditto from N.S.Y. 1 case from N.S.Y JRB	
16-2-15	"	14 Suspect Mange cases sent to Blaize Hosp. Received 2 from 1st D 6th Lancers which were found by Major McIlgois + Pepinghe JRB	
19-2-15	"	Col Bell Irvine with transport to go to Vety Hospital. 9 Suspects mange cases + 2 others passed from 5th Dragoons. Major Barry + Martin visited Section JRB	
20-2-15	"	Wrote to Genl Ollivanty who did not call. 8 mice + antiparities unsolicited against estine Received 3 cases from R.H.A. JRB	

WAR DIARY
or
INTELLIGENCE SUMMARY
(Erase heading not required.)

Army Form C. 2118.

Instructions regarding War Diaries and Intelligence Summaries are contained in F. S. Regs., Part II. and the Staff Manual respectively. Title pages will be prepared in manuscript.

Hour, Date, Place	Summary of Events and Information	Remarks and references to Appendices
21-2-15 MORBECQUE	Received 2 horses from M.S.Y. JRB	
23-2-15 "	Major Barry inspected horses in Place & gave orders that "cases" horses were to be reported to him & sent on return to Units by order of A.H. & 2. M.G. also horses dead & destroyed to be notified to Units to return on A.F.A. 2010. JRB	
24-2-15 "	Eight horses sent to Base hospital Cov. Private Mullines. JRB	
25-2-15 "	Two horses " JRB	
26-2-15 "	Two cases received from F. Hussars 3 discharged to M Boyle under instructions from A.A. & Q.M.G. through Major Barry	
27-2-15 "	Orders A.O.V.S. Major Callan & inspected horses & harness. JRB Major Marshe inspected horses, cold & had to many on hand, ordered some to Base & others to regiments. JRB	
28-2-15 "	Sent 4 15 horses to Base, discharged to 5 & 3rd Dragoons 3 to next Gen. 3 to F. Hussars (Cr. Sergt. Jemmany said he accepts horses under protest several show Keat to G.O.C. 8th Cav. Bde to harness. JRB	

1247 W 3299 200,000 (E) 8/14 J.B.C. & A. Forms/C. 2118/11.

Confidential.

War Diary

of

13th Mobile Veterinary Section.

3rd Cavalry Division.

Vol II

from 1st Mar. 1915. to 31st Mar. 1915.

Army Form C. 2118.

WAR DIARY
or
INTELLIGENCE SUMMARY
(Erase heading not required.)

Instructions regarding War Diaries and Intelligence Summaries are contained in F. S. Regs., Part II. and the Staff Manual respectively. Title pages will be prepared in manuscript.

Hour, Date, Place	Summary of Events and Information	Remarks and references to Appendices
1. Mar. '15. Morbecque.	Remain billeted at farm of Mme Coleantin Morbecque. Received our own Suspected Mange from Signal Troop N° 2, 6th Cav. Bde. JRE	
2 " '15 do	Major Pollier, acting A.D.V.S. called & inspected Mange case received yesterday. 27 Horses from Great Germany received, each by O.C. 4th Cav. Bgde. 2 " " 3rd Dragoons recvd. Sadeky was sent with the 27 horses of the Great Germany by order of his Adjutant. I accepted this under protest & without responsibility, informing Cpt Wingelrent, V.O. of the Regiment that he would have to arrange for collection of same. JRE	
3 " '15 do	Major Martin. D.D.V.S. Cavalry Corps called & inspected horses from Great Germany. 1 Case suspected mange received from Supply Officer, 6th Cav. Bde. JRE	
4 " '15 do	Received 6 horses from Rt Horse Guards, 4 from 1st Royals, 1 from I Dragoons. Major Pollier called & inspected these horses. 3 " Horses sent to Base Vety Hospital, Neufchatel. JRE 1 Horse (pneumonia) received from I Dragoons. JRE	
5 " '15 do		
6 " '15 do	19 Cast horses received from I Dragoons. Majors Martin & Pollier inspected these horses, instructing us to retain four for treatment & evacuate remainder. JRE	
7 " '15 do	Informed by Hd Qrs to be ready to move at one hours notice & made necessary preparations. JRE	

WAR DIARY
or
INTELLIGENCE SUMMARY

(Erase heading not required.)

Instructions regarding War Diaries and Intelligence Summaries are contained in F. S. Regs., Part II. and the Staff Manual respectively. Title pages will be prepared in manuscript.

Hour, Date, Place	Summary of Events and Information	Remarks and references to Appendices
8 Mar. '15. Morbecque	Received 1 horse from 8th Cav. Bde. Hd. Qrs. 8 from I Division. 1 from R. Horse Gds. Major Pallin called to inspect these. JRB	
9 " '15 "	26 Horses sent to Base Vety Hospital, Neufchatel. JRB.	
10 " '15 "	Received 6 Horses from 3rd Dragoons. 1 from 6th Cav. Bde. F.A. 2 from Scouts Group. 1 from 1st Royals. Major Pallin called to inspect these. Major Martin called later. JRB	
11 " '15 "	1 Horse received from 3rd Dragoons. 4 from 1st Royals. 4 from H. Somrivall [?] Yeomen. 8 Horses sent to Base Vety Hospital, Neufchatel. JRB.	
12 " '15 "	In view of early move all sick horses on hands (38) sent to Neufchatel. 37 to Hospital. 1 to Remounts. Allotted 2 horse lifts in relief by R. Horse Gds. [?] SRB	
13 " '15 "	Moved section to de Sart. Mr Murphy per mdev [?] 6th Cav. Bde. about an hour after arrival was ordered to return to billets at Morbecque again & did so, arriving at 7.20 p.m. Was informed that No 30 Vety Section had arrived & was attached to 7th Cav. Bde., whose horses I had hitherto been evacuating in addition to the 6th Cav. Bde. JRB.	
" '15 "	3 Cast & 3 Sick horses received from 1st Royals. Major Martin called. JRB.	

WAR DIARY
or
INTELLIGENCE SUMMARY
(Erase heading not required.)

Army Form C. 2118.

Hour, Date, Place	Summary of Events and Information	Remarks and references to Appendices
15 Mar. '15. Mortlecque.	4 Horses received from 3rd Dragoons. JRB	
16 " '15 "	2 Horses received from C. Bat. R.H.A. + 14 cast from N.Somerset Yeomanry. JRB	
17 " '15 "	1 horse in foal received from N.S.Yeomanry, Major Martin called to inspect + ordered 17 cast + 1 sick the sent to Base, remainder to be treated by Section. The 24 horses were sent to Schelsdale to-day. JRB Major Barry also called today. Collected 2 horses left on letter by Armour Col. R.H.A. JRB	
18 " '15 "	Treated horses left at Stenbecque stn by R.H.A. as per instructions from Major Martin. JRB	
19 " '15 "	1 Horse received fm C Bat. R.H.A. + 1 from N.S.Yeomanry. JRB	
20 " '15 "	Destroyed horse left at Stenbecque Stn, by request of Major Martin. JRB	
21 " '15 "	11 Cast horses received from N.Somerset Yeomanry, one of who was badly kicked while here. had leg broken (radius) + I destroyed it. Majors Barry + Martin inspected + detained horse from N.Somerset Yeomanry with badly injured knee. JRB	
22 " '15 "	22 Cast horses received from 3rd Dragoons + were inspected by Major Barry. 16 Horses sent to Base City Hospital. JRB	

Army Form C. 2118.

WAR DIARY
or
INTELLIGENCE SUMMARY

(Erase heading not required.)

Instructions regarding War Diaries and Intelligence Summaries are contained in F. S. Regs., Part II. and the Staff Manual respectively. Title pages will be prepared in manuscript.

Hour, Date, Place	Summary of Events and Information	Remarks and references to Appendices
24 Mar '16. Morbecque.	3 horses received from 1st Bayado. 22 horses cast Newfchatel. JRR.	
25 " '16 "	2 horses received from 1st Bayado. Major Marlin called. JRR.	
26 " '16 "	3 horses received from 1st Bayado. JRR.	
27 " '16 "	Inspected saddlery & rifles & ascertain started quantity of ammunition &c for retention on the Subject. JRR. Received 1 horse for treatment from 6th C.B. N° 2in Transport. JRR.	
28 " '16 "		
29 " '16 "	Received 2 horses from 3rd Dragoons. Lt. Birt. R.N. to Base Vet. Hospital Newchatel. JRR.	
30 " '16 "	Had instructions from Major Barry that I was to take charge, as V.O. of 6th Cav Bde Field Amb: A & B Echelons. 9th Cav Bde. Field Amb A+B Echelons also B Echelon of 8th Cav Bde. F. Amb. JRR.	
31 " '16 "	Major Barry called & inspected sick lines. JRR.	

Confidential.

War Diary

of the

13th Mobile Veterinary Section.

from 1st April '15 to 30th April '15.

Vol III

12/5195

'...LE' CYANIDE
...WOOL
...nd   3/-

..., SON & SONS,
...RDON, ENGLAND.

Army Form C. 2118.

WAR DIARY
or
INTELLIGENCE SUMMARY
(Erase heading not required.)

Instructions regarding War Diaries and Intelligence Summaries are contained in F. S. Regs., Part II. and the Staff Manual respectively. Title pages will be prepared in manuscript.

Hour, Date, Place	Summary of Events and Information	Remarks and references to Appendices
1-4-15. Moheerque.	Collected at farm of W.m Cadzow. Received 2 horses from 1st Royals.	
	+ 2 forks of Came harness. JRR	
2- " -15	Youths all horses of B Sqdn horses b¹, t⁴, r⁵ C.o. Rds. JRR	
3- " -15	" A 6ᵗʰ C.o. Rds JRR	
4- " -15	Received one lame cast for cart from Hd Qs 1ˢᵗ Co. Rds. JRR	
5- " -15	" from b³/ Saddle Hd Qs. " 2 " from 1ˢᵗ Royals. JRR	
6- " -15	Sent 7 horses to Base Vety Hospital. JRR	
	Received one horse from C¹/O⁴ᵗʰ R.H.A. + from 3 Dragoons. 3 from 1ˢᵗ Royals.	
7- " -15	Visited Echelon B. various Ambulances JRR	
8- " -15	Received 4 horses from 17 Sqdn. Sent 8 horses to Base Vety Hosp dos JRR	
9- " -15	" 12 " M John Thomas JRR.	
10- " -15	Inspected horses at Hd Qs 6ᵗʰ Co. Rds. 1 horse mid t/Hd Qs 6ᵗʰ Co. Rds cured JRR	
11- " -15	Received 3 horses from T Squad. Horn 6 horses sent Base V¹y Hosp. JRR	
12- " -15	Visited General W.D.S. 6, 7, + 8 Co.Rds. 1 horse pd cured 4ᵗʰ Co.Rds. R.H.A.JRR	
13- " -15	Major Pusey R.C.V.S. inspected Echelon mounts, + with wagon garrison. JRR	
14- " -15	Major Martin D.V.S. accompanied by Major Casey inspected the Echelon mounts	
	+ packed. three presents from M. Sm & Vinson JRR	
15- " -15	6 horses received from 3ʳᵈ Dragoons. 12 men inoculated against enteric	
	all mounts of Echelon are not inoculated JRR	

WAR DIARY
or
INTELLIGENCE SUMMARY
(Erase heading not required.)

Army Form C. 2118.

Instructions regarding War Diaries and Intelligence Summaries are contained in F. S. Regs., Part II. and the Staff Manual respectively. Title pages will be prepared in manuscript.

Hour, Date, Place	Summary of Events and Information	Remarks and references to Appendices
16-4-15 Morbecque	10 horses received from 1st Bde in prep. for Hd. Qrs. 6th Cav. Bde. JRP	
17-4-15	16 horses sent Base VHA Depot. 1 delivered to 3rd Dragoons. Medical Selection	
	4 Cav 3/2 Ambulances. JRP	
18-4-15	Major Mackie D.S.V.S. inspected sick at stables, went all N.C.Os JRP	
19-4-15	Rate 1 horse to 1st Royals cased. JRP	
20-4-15	Received 3 horses from 3rd Dragoons JRP	
21-4-15	" 2 " " N. Som. Yeo.	
22-4-15	" " Rate 1h - 3rd Dragoon cased. JRP	
	Proceeded with 7 horses to Hazebrouck & company with Capt Mearns +7 men & 10/10 Sect.	
	8 being away and horses from C. Batt. R.H.A. JRP	
	Kemp Farm billet at billet in my absence	
23-4-15	12 horses received from 5th Dragoons. Returned from Bailleul with 8 horses and	
	from C. Batt R.H.A. JRP	
24-4-15	30 horses sent to Base VHA Depot Rlri. Sectors packet prepared to injure at	
	our line water. Major Mackie + Barry called. Received 4 horses from 1st Royals JRP +	
25-4-15	Cast 4 horses to Base VHly Hospital. Horse kicks leg in billet at Steenverp +	
26-4-15	"Starling" by mostly to nurse. JRP	Roughen
27/28/4-15	Proceeded with I went to 6th Cav B.Gds Robinceps, brought back one horse of	
	3rd Sparrows slightly lame, two h and one to B Sietin 3rd Dragoons Rooughen.	
	During my absence 3 horses from 3rd Dragoons + 1 from 1st Royals all cases,	
	were presented at killed. JRP	

Army Form C. 2118.

WAR DIARY
or
INTELLIGENCE SUMMARY
(Erase heading not required.)

Hour, Date, Place	Summary of Events and Information	Remarks and references to Appendices
20-4-'15 Mashrequi	Acting on instructions from O.B.V.S. I prepared to move Section N.1. the G.' of 6th Car Bde at Roseingh having proceeded as far as Noghevich. I interviewed A.D.V.S. who asked me to return with Section to Killas. The H arill horses on hand were handed over to 14 Station J.R.P.	

3rd Cavalry Division

Confidential

War Diary

13 Mobile Vety Section.

1st May '15 to 31st May '15.

Vol IV

Army Form C. 2118.

WAR DIARY
or
INTELLIGENCE SUMMARY
(Erase heading not required.)

Instructions regarding War Diaries and Intelligence Summaries are contained in F. S. Regs., Part II. and the Staff Manual respectively. Title pages will be prepared in manuscript.

Hour, Date, Place		Summary of Events and Information	Remarks and references to Appendices
Morbecque.	1-5-'15	Billet. Mr Calvotti, Morbecque. Proceeded with a Sergt. to Meux to meet Capt Harris of 4th Section with whom I proceeded to Poperinghe to collect sick horses.	
do.	2-5-'15	1 horse from 3rd Dragoons received at Rest during my absence. JRB.	
do.	3-5-'15	Returned from Poperinghe with 2 horses from 1st Somerset Yeom. 1 from Hd. Qr. 6th C.O. + 1 from 3rd Dragoons. 1 Horse ret'd cured to 3rd Dragoons. JRB	
do.	4-5-'15	1 Case Surgs. shew divisional picket from 3rd Dragoons Major Barry called to inspect sick horses, ordered 2 shew cases sick and to Base Hosp. + 1 Kh. returned to 3rd Dragoons. Polish horses at Hd. Qr. 6th Cav. Bde. JRB.	
do	4-5-'15	Major Martin DDVS. called + inspected sick horses 1st + Cavs suspects. shew divisional sick Base Hospital. + 1 Pitch to 3rd Dragoons. JRB.	
do.	5-5-'15	Visited 6th 7th + 8th Field Ambulance horses + Hd. Qr. 6th C.B. JRB	
do.	6-5-'15	1 Horse received from 3rd Dragoons. Major Barry called. Return visit to Major Barry of all horses distributed by the section since arrival in the country total amount 1190. JRB	
do	7-5-'15	1 Sgt. received from 1st + 2nd Welsh Regt. JRB	

WAR DIARY
or
INTELLIGENCE SUMMARY

(Erase heading not required.)

Army Form C. 2118.

Instructions regarding War Diaries and Intelligence Summaries are contained in F. S. Regs., Part II. and the Staff Manual respectively. Title pages will be prepared in manuscript.

Hour, Date, Place	Summary of Events and Information	Remarks and references to Appendices
Molteque 8 – 5 –'15.	1 Horse received from 1st Royal Dragoons. Major Barry calls during my absence at Hd Qrs 6th C.B. 1 Capt. Received from no 9 Vety Sect. JRP	
9 – 5 –'15.	3 Horses received from N. Somerset Yeomanry. JRP	
10 – 5 –'15.	1 Horse received from 3rd Dragoons & 2 from N. Somerset Yeom. 1 of Roller cast for Vice by OC. JRP	
11 – 5 –'15.	4 horses received from 1st Royals & 1 from 3rd Dragoons. Major Barry inspects sick horses & orders 15 to be evacuated. JRP	
12 – 5 –'15.	15 horses sent to Base Vety Hospital. Major Martin A.D.V.S. called with Col. Yardley D.F.D.V. JRP	
13 – 5 –'15.	Visited horses 4 & 6 & 7 & 8th Cav. Fd Ambulance & Hd Qrs 6th Cav Bde. JRP	
14 – 5 –'15.	2 horses received from 3rd Dragoons. JRP	
15 – 5 –'15.	" " " 1st Royals. JRP	
16 – 5 –'15.	" " " 3rd Dragoons. JRP	
17 – 5 –'15.	Major Barry inspected sick horses & ordered the evacuation of 8, these were sent away at once. JRP	
18 – 5 –'15.	5 horses received from 3rd Dragoons. JRP	
19 – 5 –'15.	8 " " 1st Royals. Majors Master & Barry called & ordered the evacuation of 13 horses. JRP	

Army Form C. 2118.

WAR DIARY
or
INTELLIGENCE SUMMARY

(Erase heading not required.)

Instructions regarding War Diaries and Intelligence Summaries are contained in F. S. Regs., Part II. and the Staff Manual respectively. Title pages will be prepared in manuscript.

Hour, Date, Place	Summary of Events and Information	Remarks and references to Appendices
Morbeque 20-5-15	1 Invalid received into Vety Hospital.	
" 21-5-15	13 Horses evacuated to Base Vety Hospital. Visits paid at 6ᵗʰ, 7 & 8ᵗʰ Cav Fd Ambulances & No 2 & 6ᵗʰ Cav Bdes. JRR	
" 22-5-15	Received 1 Horse from 8ᵗʰ Cav Fd Amb.ᶜ JRR	
" 23-5-15	" 1 " 3ʳᵈ Dragoons. Major Bony inspected sick horses JRR	
" 24-5-15	8 horses sent Base Vety Hospital. JRR	
" 25-6-15	1 man in foal received from St Sans Yemn. takes as man foal during the night. JRR	
" 26-5-15		
" 27-5-15	5 horses received from St Emmund Yemn. Visits horses at 6ᵗʰ, 7 & 8ᵗʰ Cav Fd Ambulances. Major Martin acted during my absence. JRR	
" 28-5-15	Major Bony called & inspected sick horses. JRR	
" 29-5-15	6 horses evacuated from Base Vety Hospital. 1 Shoeing Smith received from No 5 Vety Hospital, & my Cpl S Smith transferred to No 2 Vety Hospital. JRR	
" 30-5-15	2 Horses received from 8 Cav Fd Amb. 1 Sgt & 1 Cpl transferred to No 10 Vety Section. JRR	

WAR DIARY
or
INTELLIGENCE SUMMARY
(Erase heading not required.)

Army Form C. 2118

Instructions regarding War Diaries and Intelligence Summaries are contained in F. S. Regs., Part II. and the Staff Manual respectively. Title pages will be prepared in manuscript.

Hour, Date, Place	Summary of Events and Information	Remarks and references to Appendices
Montreuil 31-5-15.	1 horse cart to view from 8th Can. Fd. Contn. sent to Fd. Remount, Rheims by order Col Yardley. JRP.	

3rd Cavalry Division.
Confidential.

War Diary.

13 Mobile Vety Section.

1st June '15 to 30th June '15.

Vol V

WAR DIARY
or
INTELLIGENCE SUMMARY
(Erase heading not required.)

Army Form C. 2118.

Instructions regarding War Diaries and Intelligence Summaries are contained in F. S. Regs., Part II. and the Staff Manual respectively. Title pages will be prepared in manuscript.

Hour, Date, Place	Summary of Events and Information	Remarks and references to Appendices
Shoeburyness 1 – 6 – '15.	Billed at Wm Calcutta. Shoeburyness. 4 horses received from 1st Royals. JRB	
" 2 – 6 – '15.	Major Martin called with C/S Yardley JRB	
" 3/4 – 6 – '15.		
" 5 – 6 – '15.	2 Cad Horses received from St Omer Yeom. 2 horses sent to 7th Remounts, Shirness. JRB	
" 6 – 6 – '15.	Major Berry called & ordered the evacuation of 7 6-horses. these were sent away at once. JRB	
" 6 – 6 – '15.	Specialists & Farriers & duentation personnel to as per instructions from Major Martin, returned with 2 remounts for 1st Royals. + 1 sufferer from pneumonia. JRB Received 3 horses from Sig. Troop, C.C. M^d Div.	
" 7 – 6 – '15	1 " " St Omer Yeom. Major Berry. JRB Inspection 3rd Dragoons horses with Major Berry.	
" 8 – 6 – '15	1 horse received from 3rd Dragoons. ? Removal, permission received re C.C. M^d Div. the 6th inst. dist. JRB	
" "	1 " " C Batt. R.H.A.	
" 9 – 6 – '15	2 " " "	
	5 horses and Bearer Vally dogs. Major Berry called & proceeded with him & inspected horses of 1st Royal Dragoons. St Somerset Stores. JRB	

WAR DIARY or INTELLIGENCE SUMMARY

Army Form C. 2118.

(Erase heading not required.)

Instructions regarding War Diaries and Intelligence Summaries are contained in F. S. Regs., Part II. and the Staff Manual respectively. Title pages will be prepared in manuscript.

Hour, Date, Place	Summary of Events and Information	Remarks and references to Appendices
Morbecque 9-6-15.	The following 'Cast' horses received.	
	14 from 1st Royal Dragoons.	
	15 " 3rd Dragoons.	
	14 " C Batty R.H.A.	
	2 " Hd Qrs 6th C.B.	
	8 " N. Somerset Yeom. Total. 50.	
	These were later inspected by Col. Yardley, Major Barry & the Sub Major 6th Cav. Bde. (Lt Yardley ordered 17 h.h. cast to Field Remts) JRB	
	Returns of 32 to War Rly Hospital. JRB	
10-6-'15.	1 horse received from 1st Royals.	
"	20 " " N. Som. Yeom.	
"	27 Horses sent to Base Rly Hospital.	
"	18 " " Le Rumming, Reserve	
	Major Martin & Col Yardley called & inspected horses received to day & ordered 6 cases suspicious skin disease to be returned for treatment remainder to be evacuated. JRB	
11-6-'15.	2 horses received from C.C. Hd Qrs. & 1 horse collected in Hazebrouck	
	left behind by 12th Reserve A.S.C.	
	10 horses sent to Base Rly Hospital.	
	1 Section horse lines together patients destroyed. JRB	

WAR DIARY
or
INTELLIGENCE SUMMARY
(Erase heading not required.)

Army Form C. 2118.

Instructions regarding War Diaries and Intelligence Summaries are contained in F.S. Regs, Part II. and the Staff Manual respectively. Title pages will be prepared in manuscript.

Hour, Date, Place	Summary of Events and Information	Remarks and references to Appendices
Morbecque 12-6-15.	Proceeded to Hazebrouck & dis entrains presents & brought back 1 horse from Bdo Yeomanry adjoining from Pneumonia. JRB	
13-6-15	Received 1 horse from C. Batt. R.H.A. + 1 from 8th Cav Fd Amb. JRB	
14-6-15	Destroyed horse received on the 11th hired from A.S.C. Visited 6th, 7th & 8th Cav Fd Ambulances & Hd Qrs 6th C.B. Received 15 cases mange skin disease from 1. Som. Yeom. also 2 " " 3rd Dragoons 5th Dragoons 3 " " 1 " " also 2 horses 3rd Dragoons + 2 Hd Qrs 2nd C.C. + 1 from I Hussars + 1 skin case I Hussars + 2 from 1st Royals. JRB	
15-6-15	Received 2 cast + 2 sick horses from Hd Qrs 2nd Cav. Corps. Major Morton & Col Yardley called, instructions re 5 cases skin disease for treatment + evacuate remainder. JRB Major Barry called & instructed me to purchase land & gratify + own skin cases. JRB	
16-6-15	2 horses sent to Fd. Remounts, Ruminac 1 " " Base Vety Hospital JRB	
17-6-15.		
18/19-6-15.		
20-6-15.	1 Horse received from 1st Royals. + 1 from J Batt. R.H.A. JRB	
21-6-15	1 " " 1t Som. Yeom. 21 from Hd. 2nd 6th C.B. 6th C.B. JRB	

WAR DIARY
or
INTELLIGENCE SUMMARY

(Erase heading not required.)

Army Form C. 2118.

Instructions regarding War Diaries and Intelligence Summaries are contained in F. S. Regs., Part II. and the Staff Manual respectively. Title pages will be prepared in manuscript.

Hour, Date, Place	Summary of Events and Information	Remarks and references to Appendices
Molinghem 21-6-15	Visits 6th 7th & 8th Cav. Fd Ambulances & Hd 2nd & 6th Cav Bdes. JRB	
" 22-6-15	Received 1 horse from 1st Royals & 1 from St Sson Yeom. JRB	
" 23-6-15		
" 24/25-6-15		
" 26-6-15.	3 horses received from 1st Royals & 1 from St Sson Yeom. JRB	
" 27-6-15	Visits Hd 2nd & 6th Cav Bde. JRB	
" 28-6-15.	Lieut Taggart, Major Martin & Barry inspects Gestines r. JRB	
" 29-6-15	1 horse received from 1st Royal Dragoons & 1 from 8th Cav Fd Amb. 1 horse sent to Base Vety Hospital. JRB	
" 30-6-15	Visits 6th 7th & 8th Cav Fd Ambulances. JRB	

3rd Cavalry Division

121/6390

Confidential

War Diary.

No. 13 Mobile Vety Section.

1 July 1915.   to   31st July 15.

Vol VI

F'scap paper
(as requested)

96/13th M.V.S.

X

1 of 2

Army Form C. 2118.

WAR DIARY
or
INTELLIGENCE SUMMARY
(Erase heading not required.)

Instructions regarding War Diaries and Intelligence Summaries are contained in F. S. Regs., Part II. and the Staff Manual respectively. Title pages will be prepared in manuscript.

Hour, Date, Place	Summary of Events and Information	Remarks and references to Appendices
July 1st/15	Billeted at the farm Vte Boitoulle, Morbecque.	JRS
" 2 "	Received 160 horses from 1st Royals. York Section to Ronquir at Aire for firing practice.	JRS
" 3 "	Received 1 horse from 3rd Dragoons. Visited 6th Cav. Fd. Amb. horses A+B Echelons.	JRS
" 4 "	Wrote Hd 2d ink any intention to arranged agreement with the farmer Boitoulle as to payment for use of fields at my billet.	JRS
" 5 "	Visited horses at 4th, 5th + 6th Cav. Fd. Ambulances. B Echelons.	JRS
" 6 "	Sent 8 horses to Base Vety Hospital. Col Yardley D.A.D.R. + Col Martin visited the billets.	JRS
" 7 "	D.D.V.S. + Maj Barry A.D.V.S. visited	JRS
" 8 "	Sent 5 cases suspected skin disease to Base Vety Hospital.	JRS
" 9 "	Received 2 horses from 1 Somerset Yeom + 5 from 1st Royals.	JRS
" 10 "	" 1 " do. do. + sent 5 sick horses to Base Vety Hospital.	JRS
" 11 "	Visited horses at 6th Cav. Fd. Bde. Hd Qrs.	JRS
" 12 "	Col Yardley called at billet. Received 5 surplus horses from 1st Somerset Yeomanry + 2 sick.	JRS
" 13 "	Sent 4 horses to Base Vety Hospital. Lt Col Martin + Major Barrycalled.	JRS

WAR DIARY
or
INTELLIGENCE SUMMARY

(Erase heading not required.)

Army Form C. 2118.

Instructions regarding War Diaries and Intelligence Summaries are contained in F.S. Regs., Part II. and the Staff Manual respectively. Title pages will be prepared in manuscript.

Hour, Date, Place	Summary of Events and Information	Remarks and references to Appendices
July 14-15.	Received 2 horses from Cav. Corps. Signals. 1 Corpl. transferred to No 5 Vety Hospital Abbeville.	JRP
" 15-15	Proceeded on 7 days leave to Ireland. Lt Davis of 20 Section taking charge during my absence.	JRP
" 16-15	One sick horse left at billet by 10th Lancers & received from Transport Officer, 6th Cav. Bde. 2 Horses received from 1st Royals.	JRP
" 17-15		JRP
" 18-15	Routine	JRP
" 19-15	1 Horse received from H.Q. 2nd Cav. Corps.	JRP
" 20-15	2 " " " 1st Royals.	JRP
" 21-15	7 sick sent to Base Vety Hospital	JRP
" 22-15	1 of my sergeants transferred to No 13 Vety Hospital Boulogne. 2 horses received from 3rd Dragoons + 1 from 1st Grenard Gunnery. Returns from leave. Received 1 Sergt from Vety Hospital Rouen	JRP
" 23-15	Received 1 horse from 81st Bde. R.F.H.A. + 1 from 5th Dragoons	JRP
" 24-15	" 1 corporal from Vety Hosp. Havre.	JRP
" 25-15	a suspected case Glass disease from H.Q. 2nd + C.S. Major Beany called to inspect this + advised T.S.R. sent to Base Vety	JRP

WAR DIARY
or
INTELLIGENCE SUMMARY

(Erase heading not required.)

Army Form C. 2118.

Instructions regarding War Diaries and Intelligence Summaries are contained in F. S. Regs, Part II. and the Staff Manual respectively. Title pages will be prepared in manuscript.

Hour, Date, Place	Summary of Events and Information	Remarks and references to Appendices
26 July '15	L.Col Martin called at Office. Received 3 horses from M. Sowan Yeoms + 1 from C. Batty R.N.A.	
27 July '15	Visits Lines at 6th & 7th t.t. Can. Fd. Ambulances. Sent 10 horses to Base Vety Hospital. Attended lecture by Lt Hedley at to 14 Section.	JRP JRP
28 July '15	Visits horses at Hd Qrs 6th C.B. Received 1 horse from Hd Qrs 6th C.B.	JRP
29 " '15	Received 1 horse from Hd Qrs Can Corps & 2 from 8th Dragoons.	JRP
30 " '15	" 1 " Warwick Artillery, 2 from 5 Dragoons & 1 "	JRP
31 " '15	from Hd Qrs Can. Corps. Received 4 Cases skin disease from St Semavat Yeom. 2 cases from 1st Royals. & 4 from M. Sowan Yeomanry. Sent 13 horses to Base Vety Hospital.	JRP

121/6753

ans

3rd Cavalry Hussein

13th Hotel Vety. Lahore

Part VIII

August 15

Confidential.

War Diary.

13th Mobile Vet'y Section.

to

1 Aug. 1915.

31st Aug. 1915.

WAR DIARY
or
INTELLIGENCE SUMMARY.
(Erase heading not required.)

Army Form C. 2118.

Place	Date	Hour	Summary of Events and Information	Remarks and references to Appendices
MORBECQUE	1 8/15		Remained at billet with V.C. Cantaines of Morbecque. Visited horses at H.Q. 2nd & 6th Cav. Bde. + 6th Cav. Fd. Amb.	JRB
do	2 "		Received 2 horses from 1st Dragoons. 3 from "J" Batty. R.H.A. for treatment + 1 from "C" Batty.	JRB
do	3 "		" " " 3rd Dragoons.	JRB
do	4 "		" 1 " 3rd " & 1 from 6th Cav. Fd. Amb. Sent 11 sick horses to Base Vety. Hosp. Shortlandet.	JRB
do	5 "		" " " " " Was notified that Brigade would be moving on the 6th inst. + sent my Sergt. & Farrier to arrange district to arrange billets &c.	
do	6 "		Soaked weapons & in readiness to move early. Left Morbecque at 8 a.m. & arrived at Suzzy by Cire at 2.30 pm taking with me 10 ≡ sick horses that I had under treatment. Billetted at the farm of Mons. Pouk, Cluite & Mon. Vaillet.	JRB
Suzzy/Cire	7 "		Visited 3rd Dragoons & St Somme Yeon.	JRB
do	8 "		4 previous, 2 from M. Samuel Yeomanry. Collected 3 horses left behind by the Indian Cavalry Corps.	JRB
do	9 "		Collected 2 horses left behind by Meerut Bde. Supply Col. & received 2 from N Somm Yeom. Visited horses at 6th Cav. Fd. Amb. Major Berry A.D.V.S. calls to inspect billets &c.	JRB
do	10 "		Inspected transport horses at H.Q. 2/o.	JRB
do	11 "		Proceeded to village of Sipermont & inspect horse of farmer &c and I was notified by H.Q. 2/o that mange was prevalent there, found one case, marked the farm & notified H.Q. 2/o.	JRB

Army Form C. 2118.

WAR DIARY
or
INTELLIGENCE SUMMARY.
(Erase heading not required.)

Instructions regarding War Diaries and Intelligence Summaries are contained in F. S. Regs., Part II and the Staff Manual respectively. Title pages will be prepared in manuscript.

Place	Date	Hour	Summary of Events and Information	Remarks and references to Appendices
LIGNY-LEZ-AIRE	12/15	8	Major Barry & Lt Col Morton ADVS Cavalry Corps called at billet. Returned 4 horses cured, 5 N. Sore Yeomanry. JRP	
"	13 2/10		Collected 3 horses from 3rd Lancers, 3rd Cav Cops. & received 2 from 1st Royals. Sent 4 horses to Base Vet Hospital, Abbeville. JRP	
"	14 "		Visited horses at N° 2 & 6 Cav Fd Amb. JRP	
"	15 "		Received one horse from 1st Royals. JRP	
"	16 "		Returned 1 horse cured to 5 H Hussars. Received 3 horses from 3rd Dragoons. JRP	
"	17 "		Major Barry called & informed me that I was to take over the duties of V.O. to H'qrs 2/c "C" Batty R.H.A. Ammunition Col, 6th Cav Fd Amb. as well as to my Section & that Lieut Johnson 1st Royal Dragoons would have charge of the 3 regiments of the Brigade. 1 Mentonaemia (Bart I) received. Received 1 horse from 3rd Dragoons JRP	
"	18 "		Visited "C" Bty R.H.A. & Ammun. Col. JRP	
"	19 "		14 horses sent to Base Vet Hospital, Abbeville. 1 Horse received from 1st Royals & 1 from 4 Som Yeom. JRP	
"	20 "		1 Horse sent to Base Vet Hosp. 1 received from 2nd Royals. JRP	
"	21 "		Received 1 horse from 1st Royals & 1 from H'd 2/c. Major Carry called to inspect the Section. JRP	

WAR DIARY
or
INTELLIGENCE SUMMARY.
(Erase heading not required.)

Army Form C. 2118.

Place	Date	Hour	Summary of Events and Information	Remarks and references to Appendices
Lieny-lez-MIRE	22 8/15		1 Horse sent to Base Vety Hospital. 1 horse received from N. Som Yeomanry. Visited horses of Ammun. Col. + Hd Qrs. JRP.	
"	23 "		3 horses returned to "J" Batty. R.H.A. JRP.	
"	24 "		Received 1 horse from 3rd Dragoons. Visited "C" Batty. R.H.A. JRP.	
"	25 "		8 horses sent Base Vety Hospital. JRP.	
"	26 "		Visited 6" Cav Fd Amb. Hd Qrs + Ammunn Col. 5 horses received from 3rd Dragoons + 1 from 1st Royals. JRP.	
"	27 "		Received 2 horses from N. Som. Yeom. Lt Col Martin & Maj Barry Called. JRP.	
"	28 "		2 horses sent Base Vety Hosp. JRP.	
"	29 "		1 horse received from N. Som. Yeom & 2 from 1st Royals. JRP.	
"	30 "		8 horses sent Base Vety Hosp. Visited "C" Batty, R.H.A. JRP.	
"	31 "		Visited 6" Cav Fd Amb. 9, Hd Qrs. JRP.	

3rd Cavalry Division

Confidential

War Diary.

13th Mobile Vety Section.

1 Sept. 1915.   to   30 Sept 1915.

VIII
Vol XIII

12/7466

Army Form C.2

WAR DIARY
or
INTELLIGENCE SUMMARY.
(Erase heading not required.)

Instructions regarding War Diaries and Intelligence Summaries are contained in F.S. Regs., Part II and the Staff Manual respectively. Title pages will be prepared in manuscript.

Place	Date	Hour	Summary of Events and Information	Remarks and references to Appendices
Signy by Aire	1 Sep 15		Visited horses at 6th Cav Fd Amb. & "O" Batty R.H.A. JRP	
"	2.15		Routine. JRP	
"	3.15		Received 3 horses from 3rd Dragoons. Visited horses at No. 20. JRP	
"	4.15		Visited O Batty, Ammunition Col. & 16th Fd. Amb. JRP	
"	5.15		Major Henry A.D.V.S. called at Section. JRP	
"	6/7.15		—	
"	8.15		Received 5 cases suspected skin disease from Indurance. Cav. Corps Vet. Section Hosp. Moolin called in reference to same. JRP	
"	9.15		Received 1 horse from M.M.P. 1st Cav Bde. JRP	
"	10.15		" 4 " " 3rd Dragoons. Visited all units re any change. JRP	
"	11.15		" 25 " " 3rd Dragoons mostly cast. 17 from 1st Royal Dragoons 8 from N. Som Yeomanry. JRP	
"	12-14.15		—	
"	15.15		Received 1 horse from 6th Cav Fd Hosp. No. 20. JRP	
"	14.15		Cast 22 Sick horses & 33 Cast to No 10 BV H. Shoeburyness. May Rainy called at Section. JRP	
"	15.15		Visited 1 Cav Bde Hd Qrs & Ambulances. JRP	
"	16/17.15		—	
"	18.15		Received 1 horse from 1st Royal Dragoons. 3 from Comm Yeom. 3 from 3rd Dragoons. JRP	

WAR DIARY
or
INTELLIGENCE SUMMARY.

(Erase heading not required.)

Army Form C. 2118

Instructions regarding War Diaries and Intelligence Summaries are contained in F. S. Regs., Part II and the Staff Manual respectively. Title pages will be prepared in manuscript.

Place	Date	Hour	Summary of Events and Information	Remarks and references to Appendices
Ligny ly Aire	19 8/15	—	Bivouac 3 horses from 1st Brigade.	
"	20 "		Left Ligny by bus with my "A" Echelon, joined "A" Echelon of Brigade arrived at Bois du Bienon 12.20 a.m. by B Echelon	
			proceed to Ligny in charge of the Major. JRB	
Bois du Bienon	21 "	A. Echelon	Visits C. Batty & Ammunition Col. Bivouac 2 days from Rubino. JRB	
Ligny by Aire	21 "	B "	Rest 24 Guide horses to the 10 B.V.H. Infantrill & then proceed to Hertshouts Belain. JRB	
Bois du Bienon	22 "	A "	Rest lost horses the 26 took to my B Echelon. Visits the Dr. "C" Batty & Amm Col. JRB	
Hertshouts	22 "	B "	Received 2 horses from 1st Brigade. no mounts to mount left with M.— Ebbs Hertshouts. JRB	
Bois du Bienon	23 "	A "	Visits A.D.V.S. Horse patrouied from B Echelon. JRB	
Hertshouts	23 "	B "	Major Brey called & authorized Bugr on charge topress R.F.2000 of B Echelon 6 & 2° Brigades. Lt. Col. Martin called.	
			Sent 1 mounts man to A Echelon JRB	
Bois du Bienon	24 "	A "	Received 1 mounts man from B. Echelon. Boyd 12 horses at Cheagues. On patrouie for Railhead who	
			ordered to "Bluets". Received 1 horse from R.S.m. Jones. JRB	
Hertshouts	24 "	B "	3 men sent from M.V.H. & 2 men m B "A" Echelon. JRB	
Bois du Bienon	25 "	A "	Ready to move at 6.30 a.m. as arranged to Hornet le Mines & Kernes & Vermelles. Met A.D.V.S. at Noye le Mines. JRB	
Hertshouts	25 "	B "	Men to Banques. JRB	

WAR DIARY or INTELLIGENCE SUMMARY.

Army Form C. 2118

Instructions regarding War Diaries and Intelligence Summaries are contained in F.S. Regs., Part II. and the Staff Manual respectively. Title pages will be prepared in manuscript.

(Erase heading not required.)

Place	Date	Hour	Summary of Events and Information	Remarks and references to Appendices
Rouquier	No. 9/15		A Echelon. On the move all day, returned to Mount les Mines at night. Sent to Rouen 2 Lorries & Mr 2 Perkins. Capt in charge Lawrence and another debits & premiers K.D.Y.H. with the horses JRP	
Roisel les Mines	26 "		B " Work on 2 lorries of 81st Co. A.S.C. Transferred 1 & 3rd Grooms & 1 B-Type to A.S.C. JRP	
Roisel les Mines	27 "		A " Met Lieut Davis, 20th M.T Evelon at Station. Unites Amm Col & Regt of the Brigade JRP	
Roisel les Mines	27 "		B " Collected 1 horse left by Leicester Yeom. at Doleen JRP	
Roisel les Mines	28 "		A " Lost man 33 horses from 1st Car Pol. + 6/5 Men fr Lt.5 B.V.H. Ablainville JRP	
Rouquier	28 "		B " Billetted H. Echelon under canvas near Khai winter. Capt Richardson A.V.C arrived & take charge B Echelon J. Denvere JRP	
Roisel les Mines	29 "		A " Moved to Bois des Dames and R.D.V.S. troops to the Divisional troops JRP	
Quiévie	29 "		B " 1 Man arrived from B.V.H. + 1 Reinforcement. hot out to A Echelon. JRP	
Roisel les Mines	30 "		A " Moved to Rollock in Bruay, + received 4 horses from the Brigade JRP	
Rouquier	30 "		B " Received 1 horse from 3rd B. Li. JRP	

121/7493

3rd Cavalry Division

Confidential

War Diary

13th Mobile Vety Section.

Vol IX

1 Oct. 1915. to 31 Oct. 1915.

Army Form C. 2118

WAR DIARY
or
INTELLIGENCE SUMMARY.
(Erase heading not required.)

Instructions regarding War Diaries and Intelligence Summaries are contained in F.S. Regs., Part II. and the Staff Manual respectively. Title pages will be prepared in manuscript.

Place	Date	Hour	Summary of Events and Information	Remarks and references to Appendices
Bercau	1915 1 Oct		Col. Pearson 2O/KS called. Major Barry and a horse from M.M.P. 3rd Cav Div. for evacuation. Sent 8 horses L.B.V.H. from Bapaume. JRP	
Bapaume	1 Oct		B. Echelon. Rec'd 2 horses from British Exp., 1 from 1st Royals. JRP	
Bapaume	2 "	A.	Visits Divisional troops. Met A.D.V.S. going L.G. Echelon. Col. Pearson called. Returned no of sick sand colic. 2 horses received from No. Sam Horse. JRP	
Bapaume	2 "	B.	Received 1 horse from Essex Yeo. & 2 from "C" Batty R.H.A. Sent 8 horses b. 19/10 B.V.H. Hautchstel. JRP	
Bray	3 "	A.	Move to Fosseux, new address 4.A.D.V.S. Visits horses at Dieneman Hd. 20. Received 1 horse 3rd Dragoon. JRP	
Bapaume	3 "	B.	Called to collect a horse at I Echelon left by Armoured Car, found horse had been destroyed.	
Fosseux	4 "	A.	Received 6 horses from 3rd Dragoons. Visits 2nd Vet Supplies R.F. JRP	
Bapaume	4 "	B.	Major Barry called. JRP	
Fosseux	5 "	A.	Reps. 6 horses at Bellen for Hautchstel. Visits A.D.V.S. JRP	
Bapaume	5 "	B.	Orders to stand to. JRP	
Fosseux	6 "	A.	Visits "C" Batty Horse Col. & Hd. 2rs 3rd Cav Div. Major Barry called. B Echelon arrived. 2 horses received from 1st Royals. JRP	
Fosseux	7 "	A.	1 horse received from 3rd Dragoons. + 2 from 1st Royals. Visits 2nd Cav 2nd Amb. + Hd 2rs 6th C.B. JRP	
"	8 "		Received 1 horse Hd 2rs 6th C.B. JRP	

WAR DIARY
or
INTELLIGENCE SUMMARY.
(Erase heading not required.)

Army Form C. 2118

Instructions regarding War Diaries and Intelligence Summaries are contained in F. S. Regs., Part II. and the Staff Manual respectively. Title pages will be prepared in manuscript.

Place	Date	Hour	Summary of Events and Information	Remarks and references to Appendices
Forfar.	9/12		Received 2 horses from 1st Royals + 1 from 3rd Dragoons. JRB	
"	10/12		Sent 8 sick horses to No. 10. V.H. Neufchatel. JRB	
"	11/12		Received 1 horse suffering from Scabies from 2nd Fd. Coy. R.E. Visited C. Batty + Ammn. Col. JRB	
"	12/12		Anthrax case suffering from Eczema. Visited the 2nd + 3rd Cav. Div. JRB	
"	13/12		Received 2 horses from 3rd Dragoons + 2 from 1st Som. Yeom. JRB	
"	14/12		" 3 " " " " "	
"	15/12		" " 1st Royals, 1 from the 2nd A.D.C. + 1 from 6th Cav. Fd. Amb. JRB	
"	16/12		" 2 " " 1st Royals, 2 from 1st Dragoon, 1 from 1st Som. Yeom. Sent 15 horses to B.V.H. Neufchatel. JRB	
"	17/12		" 1 " " Ammunition Col. Visits all the units in my charge. JRB	
"	18/12		Went to Belfort to arrange billets for my Section. JRB	
Belfort	19/12		Moved billets to Belfort. JRB	
"	20/12		Received 1 horse from Warwick Arttl. + 3 from 1st Royals. JRB	
"	21/12		" 1 " " A. Armoured Yeom. Visited A.D.V.S. at Gorges. JRB	
"	22/12		Visited C. Batty 1st B. 2's 6th C. Bde. JRB	
"	23/12		Sent my Sergt. + Ordly. a/c Town & Acting horse left by 6. Batty' R.H.A. Sent 6 horses to No. 4. H. Neufchatel. JRB	
"	24/12		Visited 6th Cav. Fd. Amb. + Ammn. Col. JRB	

WAR DIARY
or
INTELLIGENCE SUMMARY.
(Erase heading not required.)

Army Form C. 2118

Instructions regarding War Diaries and Intelligence Summaries are contained in F. S. Regs. Part II. and the Staff Manual respectively. Title pages will be prepared in manuscript.

Place	Date	Hour	Summary of Events and Information	Remarks and references to Appendices
Gorhart	25/10/17		Received 2 horses from 1st Royals. 1 from 3rd Sqn. Yeom. Sent my Cavy Interpreter H'away to Bellevis & Auchy. JRB	
	26 "		Moved Section to Auchy-au-Bois. JRB	
	27 "		Into C Batty 1st G. Batty R.H.A. JRB	
	28 "		Capt Jarvis V/R.D.V.S. called. JRB	
Auchy au Bois	29 "		Attended Casting parade & horse from Brigade. Received 1 horse from 1st Sqn. Yeom. JRB	
"	30 "		Received from 3rd Dragoons 15 horse cast & 17 sick. from 1st Royals 1 cast. from C Batty R.H.A. 2 sick. 98 cast + 10 (temporary) sick. from 1st Sqn. Yeom. 3 cast. JRB	
"	30 "		Sent 30 cast + 24 sick horses to Base Vety. Hosp. Amplebeck. JRB	

3rd Cavalry Division
CONFIDENTIAL.

War Diary
of
Nº 13 Mobile Vety. Section.

from 1st Nov. 15   to 30th Nov. 15.

Vol X

151/7862

WAR DIARY
or
INTELLIGENCE SUMMARY.
(Erase heading not required.)

Army Form C. 2

Instructions regarding War Diaries and Intelligence Summaries are contained in F. S. Regs., Part II. and the Staff Manual respectively. Title pages will be prepared in manuscript.

Place	Date	Hour	Summary of Events and Information	Remarks and references to Appendices
Querly sur Bois	1 11/15		Visited horses at 'C' & 'G' Batteries R.H.A. also No 2 & 6th Cav Fd. JRP	
"	2 "		Drew ½ Squ from Corbun & pack mules. Visited horses 6 Co. 3d Ambulance. JRP	
"	3 "		Received 6 horses from N. Sur Yeuse JRP	
"	4 "		" 1 " " 1st Royal Dragoons. Sent 16 horses to R.V.H. Hospitalich. JRP	
"	5 "		" 1 " " C. Batty R.H.A. Visited & Visited charges from C. Batty R.H.A. JRP	
"	6 "		" " " Nd 2, 6th C.B. & 2 from 3rd Dragoons. JRP	
"	7 "		Night horses at Nd 2, 6th C.B. JRP	
"	8 "		Received notification of my jointing orders from Nd Dn in case of a move. Visited horses at C & G Batteries R.H.A.	
"	9 "		Shew Fp 1000 from Bachir. Received 3 horses from 1st Royals, 2 horses from N. Som Yeom. Capt Richardson A.V.S. called. Inspected horses at 'C' 'H' 'G' Batteries. R.H.A. JRP	
"	10 "		Received 8 Cass horses from 1st Royals. Lt Col Menton A.D.V.S. called. Visited 1st Can Fd Amb. & Nd Dn 6th C.B. JRP	
"	11 "		Visits C & G Batty J. R.H.A. Received 1 horse from 1st Royals. Sent 9 sick & 12 Cass horses to No 10 B.V.H. Hospitalich. JRP	
"	12 "		Received 1 horse from N. Som Yeomany. Visits Nd 2, 6th Cav Bde. JRP	
"	13 "		" 6 " " 3rd Dragoons. Returned 1 Charger cmrd to 'C' Batty R.H.A. Visits C & G Batty R.H.A. JRP	

WAR DIARY
or
INTELLIGENCE SUMMARY.

(Erase heading not required.)

Army Form C. 2118

Place	Date	Hour	Summary of Events and Information	Remarks and references to Appendices
Auchonvillers	14/15		Received 1 horse from 1st Royals. Visited 6th Co. Fd. Ambulance. JRB	
"	15		" 1st Royals " Md. 2o. 6th Cav. Bde. JRB	
"	16		" " " " Ch. Car. Vn. Dubosqal 1 from 1st Bgde.(pneumonia) Sent to Rouen & Cas. Vty. Hospital. JRB	
"	17		Move to Officer with 6th Cav. Bde. arriving at 6 p.m. JRB	
Officer	18		Visited "C" & "J" Batteries R.H.A. Applied to Bde. Staff for new 2nd H. Groom, present being too small & unreliable.	
"			Received 1 Sgt. 1 Cpl. & Farrier in exchange from No. 12 Vty. Hospital. Sent 1 Sgt. & 1 Pte on leave to England. JRB	
"	19		Visited Hd. Qrs. 4 "C" Batty. R.H.A. Made application at Hd. Qr. for new billetting areas, present one being too small. JRB	
"	20		Visited 6th Cav. Fd. Amb. JRB	
"	21		Moved to new billetting area in Petit Beauranville. JRB	
Petit Beauranville	22		Received to horses east from 1st Royals. 1 Sergt. arrived to replace a recpt. of same promoted to Staff Sergt. JRB	
"	23		Drew 3/in 500 from St. Calais. Sent 1 Corpl. & 1 man to No. 12 Vty. Hosp. in exchange. Visited Hd. 2o. JRB	
"			acting parade of Hy. Bgll horses. Visited "C" Batty. R.H.A. JRB	
"	24		Visited Pads. Holm & Ambulance. Sergt. Howes sent to the 12 Vety. Hpl. Sgt. Ponard & Pte. Higgins returned	
"			off leave. men sent to No. 12 Vety. Hpl. completing exchange. Capt. Parker A.D.V.S. 3 Cav. Bu. made	
"			accompanied by Capt. Richardson. JRB	

WAR DIARY
or
INTELLIGENCE SUMMARY.
(Erase heading not required.)

Army Form C. 2

Instructions regarding War Diaries and Intelligence Summaries are contained in F. S. Regs., Part II. and the Staff Manual respectively. Title pages will be prepared in manuscript.

Place	Date	Hour	Summary of Events and Information	Remarks and references to Appendices
PETIT BEAURAINVILLE	25/4/15		Visited HdQrs 6 Cav Bde. 6 Cav Fd Amb C Batty RHA. Took over 2 horses from 3 B/o and 5 from 1st Royals. JRB	
	26/4/15		Visited HdQrs 4th Batty R.H.A. Evacuated 6 horses from Royals + 2 from 3 B/o to NEUFCHATEL JRB	
	27/4/15		Wired D.A.D.R. about 2 horses which were sent on line lit from 3 B/o. JRB	
	28/4/15		Recd 11 horses (cast) from 3 D.B. + one cast from 6th Signal Troop. Sent 22 cast horses to ABBEVILLE for instruction D.A.D.R. Cav Corps. A.D.V.S. 3 Cav Div visited cartn. Visited Amb. + HdQrs 6 Cav Bde. JRB	
	29/4/15		Visited Hd Qrs. 6th C.B., no damage to HdQrs. Recd 1/1000 or 1/4 Barker. JRB	
	30/4/15		+ C Batty. Hind found Complete han. Met A.D.V.S. C e 4 A.D.V.S. 3 Car Div. Inspected 2 Brought horses off C Batty sent description to DADR. As requested JRB. Recd two horses from 3 B/o JRB	

Confidential

War Diary
of
No. 13 Mobile Vety. Section

from 1st December 1915. to 31st December 1915.

Vol XI

WAR DIARY
INTELLIGENCE SUMMARY
(Erase heading not required.)

Army Form C. 2118.

Place	Date	Hour	Summary of Events and Information	Remarks and references to Appendices
PETIT BEAURAINVILLE	1/12/15		Visited Bde Hd Qrs + 6 Field Amb. Called on A.D.V.S. re returning of Pte Manser to complete establishment. Took over two horses from C Battery R.H.A. which were surplus by order of A.D.R. Cav Corps, also inspected sick horses from 1st Royals for treatment by order of A.D.V.S. 3rd Cav Div. SE 4 & 3 Pte Manser T.M. sent to Nº 12 Vety Hpl. JRS	
	2/12/15		NEUFCHATEL to complete exchange of 2 N.C.O.s + 6 Men. Visited "C" Battery R.H.A., 6th Cav Fd Amb, 1 Field Hd Qrs. My interpreter ordered to report at St. OMER and departed for FRUGES en route at 1.30 P.M. JRS	
	3/12/15		Visited Hd Qrs, sick horses, also asked about another interpreter. Visited Amb. + Detachment Vet. JRS	
	4/12/15		Started at 7 A.M. to meet Remounts for 3 Cav Div. at HARESQUEL with Supt + Foreman, returned 9.30 A.M. having left Pte Willingham in charge of horses for Pty Bde. Visited sick horses of 3rd Bde N. Somerset Yeo. Hd Qrs + C Battery R.H.A. Received three horses from 1st Royals. JRS	
	5/12/15 6/12/15		A.D.V.S. visited Section inspected horses for evacuation. Inspection of Smoke helmets. JRS Visited "C" Battery R.H.A. + called at Bde Hd Qrs. Met A.D.V.S. who advised me of inspection on 8 inst made out B. weekly certificate for Section + forwarded in first O/C. Received three horses from 1st Royals. JRS	
	7/12/15		Visited Hd Qrs Cav Bde. Took on 5 horses from 3 Bde. Mallenin his horses of 3 Bde which did not react. JRS	
	8/12/15		Present at inspection of horses by A.D.V.S. from Hd Qrs 6 L.B. C Battery + amm Col R.H.A. JRS	

WAR DIARY or INTELLIGENCE SUMMARY

Army Form C. 2118.

Place	Date	Hour	Summary of Events and Information	Remarks and references to Appendices
	9/12/15		Visits made out AF: 2000 Received 6 horses from N.C.Y. JRB	
	10/12/15		A.D.V.S. exceed inspected horses for evacuation. Mallinnes two horses from N.S.Y. made out description roll of horses. JRB	
	11/12/15	6AM	Went with Sergt 16 men to MONTREUIL STATION to meet Remounts for 3 Cav Bde returned being Sergt in charge of remounts until arrival of Regts. Evacuated 14 horses to No 13 V. Hpl NEUFCHATEL	
			Visits Bill Ad Qrs & see Horses of MMP. JRB	
	12/12/15		Visited "C" Battery RHA & inspected horses of Hd Qrs & Sec Bdes. JRB	
	13/12/15		Went to Neufchatel with A.D.V.S. to demonstration of Mallein Test at No 13 Vety Hpl Afford, knew from 3DP41/mNS7 to 500	
	14/12/15		A.D.V.S. inspected horses for evacuation, made arrangements for Mallein Test in the Bde. inspected horses for transfer at "J" Batty. JRB	
	15/12/15		Visited HdQrs "J"Batty Royals went from A.D.V.S. & made arrangements with Bol.V.O. to start testing on Friday. Evacuated 4 sick + two eaus to ABBEVILLE JRB	
	16/12/15		Visits HdQrs + "J" Batty RHA exeed to Royals with reference to Mallein Testy	
	17/12/15		Test Royals in company with Lieut Johnston Avc JRB	
	18/12/15		N. Somerset Yeo inspected Royals with Lieut Johnston AVC, Sergt + 6 men sent to MONTREUIL to meet remounts. Nine cast horses received from "J" Batty RHA JRB	

WAR DIARY or INTELLIGENCE SUMMARY

Army Form C. 2118.

Place	Date	Hour	Summary of Events and Information	Remarks and references to Appendices
PETIT BEAURAINVILLE	19/12/15			
"	20/12/15	9.AM	Tested 3 D.Q. for Glanders met A.D.V.S. at OFFIN JRS	
"	21/12/15	"	Hd Qrs 6th Res Bde + 6 Batty R.H.A. JRS Inspected Hd Qr + 6 Batty R.H.A. Remounts & Cast horses from "E" Batty R.H.A. to NEUFCHATEL ≈ 700 ex Cashin 3.C.D. JRS	
	22/12/15		PM an unexpected Glanders from Royals with A.D.V.S. 3 Cav Bde Inspected Hd Qrs 6th Bde + C Batty finished testing of Hd Qrs + 6 Batty + this Section JRS	
	23/12/15		Inspected Hd Qrs + "b" Batty R.H.A. met A.D.V.S. at 6 Batty went round Rode. inspected with him. Granted leave to Ireland. Lieut Johnston A.V.C. day duty. JRS	
	24/12/15		Two horses from N.S.Y.s for Invaculation + three suspected atrive sickness for treatment from 3 D.Gs. Took over 39 horses from 1st Royals transit to NEUFCHATEL. JS (+HAE.)	
	25/12/15	6.30AM	Sergt. Stephens + four men to met remount train at MONTREUIL. JS for A.M.oq	
	26/12/15		Took over 35 horses from 3 Bde transmitted same to NEUFCHATEL. JS (+HAE.)	
	27/12/15		Recd. from 1st Royals 1 horse (Doubtful Mallein Reac) + returned one to them (Doubtful ears) by orders A.D.V.S. JS (+HAE.)	
	28/12/15		Three returned from Royals with orders to keep it here with Section. One horse from Hd Qrs 6 Cav Bde with strangles. Luttished which was emptied to their establishment JS for HAE.	
	29/12/15		Routine JS for HAE	

2353 Wt. W2544/1454 700,000 5/15 D.D.&L. A.D.S.S./Forms/C. 2118.

Army Form C. 2118.

WAR DIARY
or
INTELLIGENCE SUMMARY.
(Erase heading not required.)

Instructions regarding War Diaries and Intelligence Summaries are contained in F. S. Regs., Part II and the Staff Manual respectively. Title pages will be prepared in manuscript.

Place	Date	Hour	Summary of Events and Information	Remarks and references to Appendices
PETIT BEAURAINVILLE	30/12/15		Took over 1 hour from 3 Dys. (As for H11e)	
	31/12/15		Took over 3 horses from 3 Dys. H.D.U.S. visited section & gave instructions for evacuation of 4 horses (suspected skin) to NEUFCHATEL H.M.J. for JC3	

Army Form C. 2118.

WAR DIARY
or
INTELLIGENCE SUMMARY.
(Erase heading not required.)

No. 13 M.V.S.

Place	Date	Hour	Summary of Events and Information	Remarks and references to Appendices
PETIT BEAVRAINVILLE	1/6	7 AM	Sergt Quickhurst + 5 men sent to MONTREUIL to meet remounts. JRS per HMG. 4 cases of Surg Skin disease sent NEUFCHATEL	
	2/6		Routine JRS per HMG	
	3/6		Received 3 horses from 3 B.Vc.	
	4/6		H.D.V.S inspected horses, received out for Royals + one for 6th Signal Troop for evacuation. JRS	
	5/6		Visited Hd.Qrs. 3 B.Vc. + N.Somerset Vc. Evacuated 5 sick + eat to 3. Skin Dn. to NEUFCHATEL. No 6440 Pte. Tugwell & grantia leave to England from 6 — 11/6. departed 6.15 P.M. had rain from A.D.V.S. 3 C.D. at 8.55 P.M. for return of pose summary batsman had left. JRS	
	6/6		Visited Hd Qrs of Bde. - 3 Bde + N.S.Vc. made round weekly returns. Gave Helmet Drill. Three horses from 3 Bde tentatively with R.field Mallein. Trotted, 1 horse from N.Y. 2 from Royals + 2 from 3 B.S. with English Mallein. JRS	
	7/6		Visited units under my charge - Rifle drill remains. JRS	
	8/6		A.D.V.S visited section inspected horses underpay Mallein Test. Sergt Stephens to Montreuil to meet remounts. Received two teams of French Mallein to french Rose. JRS.	
	9/6		Visited Fodr Sta Bvc. 3 Bde. + relieved horses of 3 Bde. JRS	
	10/6		Visited 2 Bde + N.S.Y. inspected A.Syd. No 10990 from 7th Garrison inspected Mallienid horses 3 D V s. JRS	
	11/6		A.D.V.S visited Section transported Skin Suspects of 3 Bde. Mallienied 8 horses N.S.Y and	

WAR DIARY or INTELLIGENCE SUMMARY

Army Form C. 2118.

(Erase heading not required.)

Place	Date	Hour	Summary of Events and Information	Remarks and references to Appendices
PETIT BERRAINVILLE	11/7/16 (cont)		4 horses of Rath Fd. Amb. Inspected Mallein'ed of 3 D.S. JRS.	
	12/7/16		Inspected Mallein horses N.S.Y. Fd. Hd Qrs. Visited 3 D.A.C. inspected 78 Sqn. N.S.Y. 2 horses returned to 3 Dlc, 2 horses to Royals + 1 to N.S.Y. which had been retested with English Mallein. Received 2 horses from Royals (amputation + entery). JRS	
	13/7/16		Inspected Mallein'ed horses of N.S.Y. + Ballette Qrs. visited 3 D.A.'s inspected M.R. Section. reported doubtful reactors of Polo Hd. Qrs. (Rendezvous horse) to A.D.V.S. JRS	
	14/7/16		Visited 2 D.A.'s + N.S.Y. inspected "C" Sqn N.S.Y. A.D.V.S. visited doubtful Mallein case + advised it to be retested. JRS	
	15/7/16		Inspected A. By. 3 D.A. + Train sick. visited N.S.Y. + Berks Fd Amb. Doubtful case retested. received one horse from 1st Royals. Sergt Stephens to Montreuil to meet remounts. Received wire 8.35 PM for description of horses at Mallein'ed in units under my charge. JRS	
	16/7/16		Sent description of horses to A.D.V.S. by Lieut Johnston's message at 9.25 AM. Inspected Mallein retest case + horses of Bde Hd Qrs. Inspected "A" Cy. N.S.Y. JRS	
	17/7/16		Received 4r 200 & 4r broken No. 9161 Pl. Willingham F. J. awarded 14 days F. P. N°1 for being conducted wy. stables in not grooming his horse + absence from watering stables on 13th inst.	

WAR DIARY
or
INTELLIGENCE SUMMARY.
(Erase heading not required.)

Army Form C. 2118.

Place	Date	Hour	Summary of Events and Information	Remarks and references to Appendices
PETIT BEAURAINVILLE	17/7/16 (cont)		Inspected 'B' Sqn 3 D.G. Hallein retint cases at Bde Hd Qrs JRB	
	18/7/16		A.D.V.S. visited section inspected horses for evacuation. Recd two from 3 D.G. + one from Aux. H.T. A.S.C. Visited 3 Bdrs + N.S.Y. JRB Evacuated 4 sick + 4 casualties to G N°13 V.H. NEUFCHATEL (3 Royals + 3 D.G + 1 A.S.C.)	
	19/7/16		P.M. on horse at 3 D.G. (inspection of [illegible]) JRS	
	20/7/16		Visited 3 Bdrs + N.S.Y. A.Sq. +Batt.Hd.Qrs. Sent weekly returns to A.D.V.S. Rifle Drill JRB	
	21/7/16		Visited units under my charge. Foot drill JRB	
	22/7/16	7/45 AM	Went to MONTREUIL to meet Rennards to 3 Sectns. One remount had [illegible] too bad, Y10 8th Res Bett. [arrow] the serve others which were in aunt bar [illegible] separate gave instructions to NCO i/c Party to keep it + the seven others which were in aunt bar [illegible] separate from the remainder of his horse, its report to his Farriers Major where them isolated until inspected by the V.O. I also gave him a message to be delivered to the V.O. + notified A.D.V.S. 3 bas Sce. by wire. Made arrangements with R.T.O. to have truck disinfected. D.A.D.R. cast three of my section horses which I had at Railhead. JRB	
	23/7/16	9.45	Inspected horses of Bde Hd Qrs + afterwards A. Sq. N.S.Y	
	24/7/16		Inspected remount of the 3 D.G. in company with the S.O.. Had Section Parade in marching order. Received 1 horse from Royals + 1 from Hd Qrs N Somerset Ye. Drew W 400 from Field Cashier JRB	

WAR DIARY
or
INTELLIGENCE SUMMARY.
(Erase heading not required.)

Army Form C. 2118.

Instructions regarding War Diaries and Intelligence Summaries are contained in F.S. Regs., Part II. and the Staff Manual respectively. Title pages will be prepared in manuscript.

Place	Date	Hour	Summary of Events and Information	Remarks and references to Appendices
PETIT BEAURAINVILLE	25/7 26/7		Had Kit Inspection. Received Horse from Royal troops. Visited A Sq 3 D.G. JRS. Recd 1 horse from Royale. A.D.V.S. for Corps called at Section in my absence & inspected Skin case of 3 D.G. ¾ that of the Royals which came in this morning. M/S A.D.V.S. Corps at 3 p.m. to ordered me to destroy horse of Royale unit was an old wobbler & unfit for service. Inspected H.Q. & Sq 3 D.G. awaited Bde Hd Qrs & N.S. Yeomanry sent to Montreuil for trucks but was informed could not have them until tomorrow. JRS	
	27/7		Destroyed horse of Royals. Evacuated 3 cast horses (from this Section) & two sick (one from Royale, one from N.S.Y. to NEUFCHATEL. Inspected B Sq 3 D.G. JRS	
	28/7		Visited Bde Hd Qrs & N.S.Y. & 3 D.G. Rifle Inspection & Drill. Returned one horse to Royale. JRS	
	29/7		Visited units under my charge. Inspected Remounts of 3 D.G. Did not go to MONTREUIL as I received no intimation of arrival of remounts. JRS	
	30/7		Inspected Horses of Bde Hd Qrs & A. Sq. N.S.Y. waited out of 3 D.G. JRS	
	31/7		Received 1 horse from Royals. Two from N.S.Y. Rifle drill. JRS.	

WAR DIARY
or
INTELLIGENCE SUMMARY.
(Erase heading not required.)

Army Form C. 2118.

Place	Date	Hour	Summary of Events and Information	Remarks and references to Appendices
PETIT BEAVRAINVILLE	1/2/16		Saddle inspection. Took serapings of horse of 3 D. Bn under treatment for skin disease	
	2/2/16		but failed to find parasite. Visited sick of 3 D Bn & N.S.Y. JRB. Rifle drill. Inspected B & C Sqdn. 3 By. Reported suspected skin disease in C Sq. GADVS by wire. Visited sick at N.S.Y. JRB.	
	3/2/16		A.D.V.S. inspected S. Skin Case at 6 Sqdn. 3 Div + afterwards visited Section. JRB.	
	4/2/16		Received 3 horses from N.S.Y. sent by A.D.V.S. as suspected skin cases, also 4 cast horses from 3 Bde. Visited 3D Bde sick & N.S.Y. JRB	
	5/2/16	4.15AM	M.I. remounts for 3 horses at MONTREVIL & took over 3 horses for this section to replace three cast on 22-1-16. Visited sick of 3rd D Bn & Bde HdQrs. JRB	
	6/2/16		Inspected horses of Bde HdQrs & A Sqdn. N.S.Y. JRB	
	7/2/16		Rec'd Vermond Spray from 19 V. Hosp. Rec'd two horses from N.S.Y. 3 from 1st Royals + two from 20 TMB U.S. Rec'd wire from A.D.V.S. to kill over horses until 9th inst. JRB	
	8/2/16		Rec'd 1 horse from 3 D. Bde + two from N.S.Y. Visited A.Sq. 3 Bde HdQrs. + Bde M Bns. Withopatrn. 1 BA	
	9/2/16		A.D.V.S. visited unit + afterwards inspected skin cases under observation at 3 Bde + afterwards visited section. Evacuated 5 cast horses 11 sick + one skin disease to No 13 Mob. NEUFCHATEL. Sev. of Lutn. Hunt T.J. (No 726) granted leave to England JRB	

WAR DIARY or INTELLIGENCE SUMMARY.

(Erase heading not required.)

Army Form C. 2118.

Instructions regarding War Diaries and Intelligence Summaries are contained in F.S. Regs., Part II. and the Staff Manual respectively. Title pages will be prepared in manuscript.

Place	Date	Hour	Summary of Events and Information	Remarks and references to Appendices
PETIT BEAURAINVILLE	10/2/16		Visited sick of units under my charge. Inspected B. Sg. N.S.Y. Made arrangements returns Sergt. had men at Rifle Butts. JRS	
	11/2/16		Visited sick. Were present by order of Staff Capt. at G.O.C.C. Corps' inspection of remounts at Bde Hd Qrs. Pte W. do W. N° SE 6023, returned to Section from Dismounted Role.	
	12/2/16	7·10AM	Went to MONTREUIL with Sergt & 5 men to set remounts for 3 hrs. Ben visited sick of units under my charge. Received 4 cast horses for Pte Hell..	
	13/2/16		Inspected horse of 6th C. R de Hall. A. S. g. 1st Hall. N.S.Y. & inspected horses which were with dismounted party. Destroyed horse (Chap Johthly of Smiths) of this postn 07. JRS	
	14/2/16		Inspected horse of 3 BBr which were with dismounted Role + inspected remounts of N.S.Y. with Porighen Baquell. Visited sick of units under my charge. JRS	
	15/2/16		Inspected "C" Sg. 3 D Gs + part of A. Sg. Visited sick of units under my charge. Rifle Inspection. JRS	
	16/2/16		M.M.A.D.V.S. of 3 BBr to inspect suspected skin cases, afterwards at lecture. Sergt Lutchurst T9 (N° 426) returned from leave with paro of pair of new error of mine delay. Inspected Machine G. section 3 D Gs. Received 3 horses from S.D.Bs. Inoculated Bull 1st	
	17/2/16		Horse cast + four sick evacuated. Saddle Inspection. Visits FRUGES with reference	

WAR DIARY or INTELLIGENCE SUMMARY

Army Form C. 2118.

Place	Date	Hour	Summary of Events and Information	Remarks and references to Appendices
PETIT BEAUVRAINVILLE	17/2/16		The exchange of A.S. Wagon for G.S. limber visited sick at N.S.Y. + 3 D.G. + section westerly return. JRS	
"	18/2/16		Visited units under my charge. One horse returned to Belcote Gen. Hosp. Rifle Inspection JRS	
"	19/2/16		Met D.D.V.S. Base Cote + A.D.V.S. show over Hd Qrs of 3 DGs inspected S. Skin Branche afterwards inspected S. Skin Branche at my section, then inspected Section. JRS	
"	20/2/16		Inspected horses of Blue Hussars + A. Sy N.S.Y. A.D.V.S. inspected surg. Skin case in 3rd Troop of H.S.Y. + ordered evacuation. Ordered - to be taken over on arrival at mobilisation. JRS	
"	21/2/16		One horse of N.S.Y. surg skin disease evacuated station to Base by 20 MVS. Recd. 1 horse from Royals (broken wind). Inspected horses of 3"DGs. Still JRS	
"	22/2/16		Recd. 2 horses from Royals, 3 from 3rd. H. Sg. R.E., + 2 from 3 DGs. A.D.V.S. visited section with Capt HARDING JRS	
"	23/2/16		Evacuated 4 horses to NEUFCHATEL. Visited Base Hd Qrs N.S.Y. + 30 Gs sick, Mounted Drill JRS	
"	24/2/16		Visits units ending my change made out returns A + V.S. arrival as to got 2 Bath. RHA return. JRS	
"	25/2/16		Visited L Batty inspected one of their horses, other sick, also N.S.Y. JRS	
"	26/2/16		Visited L Batty RHA + Bad Hd Qrs. received 1 horse from N.S.Y. JRS	
"	27/2/16		Inspected Base Hd Qrs + A. Sg N.S.Y. JRS	
"	28/2/16		Received 2 horses from Royals, went with Capt Bapt. to look for billets at LEBIEZ, Sgt Sexton	

WAR DIARY
or
INTELLIGENCE SUMMARY.

(Erase heading not required.)

Army Form C. 2118.

Place	Date	Hour	Summary of Events and Information	Remarks and references to Appendices
PETIT BEAVRAINVILLE	29/1/16	10.45 AM	Left PETIT BEAVRAINVILLE & started for LEBIEZ to new billeting area	
LEBIEZ	29/1/16	12.15 PM	A.D.S. arrived and inspected horses for evacuation. R.T.O. would not could not send horses away for another 24 hrs. JRS	

WAR DIARY
or
INTELLIGENCE SUMMARY.
(Erase heading not required.)

Army Form C. 2118.

Place	Date	Hour	Summary of Events and Information	Remarks and references to Appendices
LEBIEZ	1/3/16		Visited 'b' Battery R.H.A. + 3 B⁰. Breve to 1000 & the Cashier for Pay i/c at FRUGES. Rec'd 1 horse from Royals, 1 + NSY 9 + 1 from 3 H.Sy.	
	2/3/16		Visited all units under my charge + inspected 3 B⁰. G.s. Had wire to be ready to move in a few days.	
	3/3/16		Pishy equipment Evacuated air horses. JRP. One horse of Royals sent in on 2/3/16 died during night. Rec'd 3 horses from 1st Royals, + 2 from 3 H.Sy. RE. Visited M.G. Sqd. 3 B⁹.s. N.S.Y. + Bde. Hd Qrs. JPB	
	4/3/16		Visited 'b' Battery, 3 B⁰. + M.G. Squadron. Sergt Johnston sent for horse of 3 F.S. admitted yesterday. Pte. BURRELL No. 885936 reported for duty from No. 12 Vety Hosp NEUFCHATEL. JPB	
	5/3/16		Inspected Bde Hd Qrs Horses + A Sq N.S.Y. JPB	
	6/3/16		Visited "B" Battery R.H.A. N.S.Y. + 3 B⁰. Rifle Drill. JPB Drew An. 100 from the Bank.	
	7/3/16		A.D.V.S. visited section inspected horses for evacuation afterwards visited outposts of 3 B⁰.s + N.S.Y. Rec'd 2 horses from 3B⁰s one from B Batty R.H.A + one from M.G.Sqd. JPB	
	8/3/16		Evacuated 12 horses to NEUFCHATEL. Visited B Batty "B"B⁰s. Rifle inspection JP.B.	
	9/3/16		Two horses returned cured to B Bgd N.S.Y. Inspected 3 B⁰s JPB	
	10/3/16		Rec'd one horse from NSY. Visited B Battery Marching order Parade JPB	
	11/3/16		Not required at Montreuil visited with Sergt + 4 men knackers foundry horses + collection for B Battery R.H.A. which they took over in the evening. JPB	

WAR DIARY
or
INTELLIGENCE SUMMARY.

(Erase heading not required)

Army Form C. 2118.

Instructions regarding War Diaries and Intelligence Summaries are contained in F. S. Regs., Part II. and the Staff Manual respectively. Title pages will be prepared in manuscript.

Place	Date	Hour	Summary of Events and Information	Remarks and references to Appendices
LE BIEZ	12/3/16		Inspected Horses of Bde. Hd. Qrs. and visited sick of 3 D. Q. JRS	
	13/3/16		Rec'd B horses from Royale, and 1 from 3 F. Sy. R.B., per Capt Johnston, of horses from N.S.Y.	
			1 from Am. H.T. Boy 3 Ca Biv. Visited 3rd Bde. & B Batty R.HA	
	14/3/16		Have rec'd from Royale on yesterday's date, one horse N.S.Y. received yesterday taken over by Capt Johnston.	
			Rec'd Two horses from 6th Cav. Bde. Amb., 1 from 3 F. Sy. R.B., 1 from 3 Sy. Sy. R.B	
			1 from 4th Bde Amn Col., 3 from 3 Bde, 2 from N.S.Y. 1 from 6th Cav Bde H.Q. Sqd. 7 D.v.S. visited	
		2 P.M.	action accompanied by Capt Johnston.	
			Inspection by Brig-Gen. Campbell 6th Cav. Bde. in marching order. JRS	
	15/3/16		Inspected horses of 3rd D. Q. JRS	
	16/3/16		Evacuated 18 Horses to NEUFCHATEL. Sent horse ex Royale +1 ex M.G. Sq. to 14 M.V.S., demobilised	
			6 Battery R.HA. Rifle Drill. JRS	
	17/3/16		Visited Bde. Hd.Qrs. + 3rd Bde. Rifle Drill. Went to see Maire of BEAURAINVILLE with	
			reference to claims to damages. JRS	
	18/3/16		Inspects "C" Batty, visited 30% 4 Bde Mid Qr. Rifle Drill. Rec'd one horse from N.S.Y. JRS.	
	19/3/16		Inspected Bde. Hd. Qrs. visited 30% JRS	
	20/3/16		Visited "B" Batty R.HA Rec'd 4 horses from N.S.Y., 3 from Royale + 2 from 6th Cav. Bde	
			M.G. Sqd. JRS. Rec'd Mr. 5/1000 ex Hd. backer JRS	

WAR DIARY or INTELLIGENCE SUMMARY.

Army Form C. 2118.

Place	Date	Hour	Summary of Events and Information	Remarks and references to Appendices
LEBIEZ	21/3/16		A.D.V.S. Barkin accompanied by Capt Johnston inspected section in marching order. Afterwards inspected horses from reservation. Rec'd one horse from "C" Batty RHA, one from 6th How Bde HA. 2nd lieut. gone from Royals. Visited "B" Batty +3 Bdes. JRS	
	22/3/16		Inspected 3 B/5s motley Bde HdQrs Hunted hill JRS	
	23/3/16		Evacuated 14 horses to NEUFCHATEL. Visited B Batty & found suspected skin case wound A.D.V.S. JRS	
	24/3/16		Visited B Batty and A.D.V.S. Visited 3 Bdes Rec'd receiving skin diseases from "B" Batty R.H.A. Hot drill. JRS	
	25/3/16	AM 7:30	Started to meet remounts at Montreuil with 1 sergt + 10 men returned 4:30 P.M. JRS Remounts Montreuil returned 2 P.M. Sent skin case "C" Batty to NEUFCHATEL JRS	
	26/3/16	6:30	Rec'd 11 horses from Royals 2 from N.S. Yeo. 2 from 3rd D.A. 2 from M.G. A/A 5 Cav Bde. JRS	
	27/3/16		Rec'd 1 horse from 6th Cav Batt. (Roots) 1 from Aux H.T. boy, 1 from 3 Fd Tp RE + 1 from "B" Batty R.H.A. A.D.V.S. visited section & inspected horses ordered two horses be returned Royals. "B" Batty have the held over.	
	28/3/16		Rec'd 1 horse from HdQrs 6th Cav Bde, 4. 1 from HdQrs 3 Cav Bn, 1 from 4" Bde R.H.A. Amm. Col. as well as one from Aux H.T. boy, attached to Royals. JRS	

WAR DIARY
or
INTELLIGENCE SUMMARY.

Army Form C. 2118.

Place	Date	Hour	Summary of Events and Information	Remarks and references to Appendices
LEBIEZ	29/3/16 30/3/16	P.M.	On Brigade Route March returned 2.30 pm. Visited "B" Battery with M.R. Evacuated 21 horses to NEUFCHATEL returned two to ROYAL. Inspected horses of 3 Bty.	
	31/3/16		In morning & three of "B" Batty in the afternoon. J.R. Rifle instruction with "B" Batty & 3 Bty & N Bde. Hd.qrs. J.R.	

Army Form C. 2118.

WAR DIARY
or
INTELLIGENCE SUMMARY.
(Erase heading not required)

Instructions regarding War Diaries and Intelligence Summaries are contained in F. S. Regs., Part II. and the Staff Manual respectively. Title pages will be prepared in manuscript.

Place	Date	Hour	Summary of Events and Information	Remarks and references to Appendices
LEBIEZ	1/4/16		Inspected horses of 3 B.% with Morgaria & Campbell. Visited reset offPathto JRS	
	2/4/16		Inspected horses of BdeHQ drivers & Pbatty R.H.A JRS	
	3/4/16		Recd authors from N.S.Y. tentor Royals one from M.G. Sgn two from 3 D.Gds. Visited 3 D.%. drew fm 1000 & Hd. parties. Mounted Drill	
	4/4/16		Recd authors from "L" Batty. three from N.S.Y. tone from 3 F.Sq. R.E. M.D.V.S. Visited aviation hospital horse for inspection. Visited Tent Hd Qn & L Batty & inspected sight section. JRS	
	5/4/16		Proceeded 12 horses to NEUFCHATEL, Visited 3 D.%. a L Batty JRS	
	6/4/16		Visited units. was my charge & received wires. returns. d.& No 692 Recommended A pusket 3 days leave in England. F.Sd wire from 3 D.%. Ens horses had been sent to theft whilst the other 3 Pm	
			dead & back & horse died about 1½ hours after my arrival, inspected poison on CW.B.I. tsts in troop JRS	
	7/4/16		Ord. batty. Inspected by D.A.D.R. Afterwards visited 3 B%. with F.Q.V.& Field P.M on horse found stomach ruptured in both cases. Recd one horse from M.G Sqdn JRS	
	8/4/16		Recd. 21 horses from 3st Royals 18 from N.S.Y. 18 from 3 B%. 6 from M.G. Sqn all sent by D.A.D.R. & presented the Lt. (62) GABBEVILLE. took over extra horse from 3 B%. to Capt Johnston A.V.S. by order of D.A.D.R. Recd one extra horse from 6th Frizard Troop JRS	

2353 Wt. W2514/1454 700,000 5/15 D. D. & L. A.D.S.S. Forms/C 2118.

WAR DIARY
or
INTELLIGENCE SUMMARY.
(Erase heading not required.)

Army Form C. 2118.

Instructions regarding War Diaries and Intelligence Summaries are contained in F. S. Regs., Part II. and the Staff Manual respectively. Title pages will be prepared in manuscript.

Place	Date	Hour	Summary of Events and Information	Remarks and references to Appendices
KEBIEZ	9/11/16		Inspected horses of Pde.Hd.Qrs + visited 'C'Batty R.H.A. JRS	
	10/11/16		Rec'd three home (?) from H.G. Sqn. 2 from N.S.Y, 16 from 3 D.G's.	
	11/11/16		Rec'd 3 from N.S.Y. + 5 from Royals. A.D.V.S. visited section inspected horses. Visited Rifle Hd.Qrs. tried out Browning Rifle. Inspected some of horses of 3 D.G's.	
	12/11/16		Evacuated 31 horses to ABBEVILLE. Visited 3 D.G's + 'C' Batty R.H.A. JRS	
	13/11/16		Visited all units under my charge, forwarded weekly returns, inspecting some horses of 'C' Batty. Some of 3 D.G's. JRS	
	14/11/16		Fit inspection visited 3 D.G's. Rifle drill. Pte Simmonds returned from leave with signed forms showing he was detained at Rest Camp in Boulogne. JRS	
	15/11/16		Visited 'C' Batty R.H.A. + 3 D.G's. JRS	
	16/11/16		Inspected horses of Pde. Hd.Qrs. Collected two H.D. horses from Royals + two from 'C' Batty R.H.A. visited 'C' Batty. JRS	
	17/11/16		Rec'd two horses from N.S.Y.	
	18/11/16		A.D.V.S. visited Section inspected horses for evacuation. Visited 'C' Batty 3 D.G's. JRS Sent H.A.D. horses collected on 16 inst to FAQUENBERGUE'S Railway Station in charge of Sergt Stephens. Inspected 3 D.G. horses. JRS	
	19/11/16		Drew tr 1000 ct Ht Larkin JRS	

WAR DIARY
or
INTELLIGENCE SUMMARY.

Army Form C. 2118.

Place	Date	Hour	Summary of Events and Information	Remarks and references to Appendices
LEBIEZ	20/4/16		Visited all units. made my charge made out returns. Rifle drill JRB.	
	21/4/16		Visited "C" Batty R.H.A. + 3 D.B. Rec'd one Surg Shoe base from N.S.Yr. for treatment + five surplus horses from G.H.Q. W.T. Coy. JRB.	
	22/4/16		Visited Bde Hd Qrs + 3 Btts. Rec'd. in horses from Lt. GAGE, G.S. OI 3rd Bn Div by order of D.A.D.R. JRB.	
	23/4/16		Inspected horses of Bde Hd. Qrs visited "C" Batty R.H.A. Collected 3 horses left by N.Z.A.S.C. at Rest Camp near FRESSIN. JRB.	
	24/4/16		Rec'd. two horses from N.S.Yr. + 1 from 6th A.G. Ag. Mounted drill JRB.	
	25/4/16		Inspected horses of "C" Batty R.H.A. took over 1 cast horse from them. Sent one horse from G.H.Q. W.T. Coy to 6th Signal Troop by order D.A.D.R. A.D.V.S. + S.V.D.R. visited section inspected horses No S.E. + 32M S.S. TAIT. J reported to duty from No 2 Vety Hpl. JRB.	
	26/4/16		Sent two horses from G.H.Q. W.T. Coy to 8th Cav Fd Amb. one to 3 F/Sg R.S. + one to 4 Bde R.H.A. Amm Col. Visited 3 Bde of Batty R.H.A. Collected horse from Batt HOWARD at NEUVILLE. No 215 S.S. Cpl BOYNE. M. sent to duty to No 2 Vety Hpl. No 9 Rec'd one horse which was sent to 4th Bde R.H.A. Amm Col yesterday with note accpt	

WAR DIARY or INTELLIGENCE SUMMARY

Army Form C. 2118.

Place	Date	Hour	Summary of Events and Information	Remarks and references to Appendices
KEBIEZ	27/4/16		It was not available. Recd 13 Capt horses from "C" Batty R.H.A. M.H. movement-train at MONTREUIL took on a chest cher for Capt Radcliffe. Sent horse collected yesterday at NEUVILLE to C/GAGE at FRUGES. Sent two horses (cured) to A Sqn N.S.Y. 12th Sergt LUKEHURST + 4 men sent to MONTREUIL to meet remounts. Evacuated 14 cast horses from "C" Batty R.H.A. to ABBEVILLE. Sergt. Stephen Some man sent to FAQUEMBERGUES with two horses one of which was handed to Col Radcliffe R.E. + the other to 3rd Reserve Park	
	28/4/16		Recd two horses from A Sy N.S.Y. Capt. Ellison A.V.C. went on leave Capt Johnson A.V.C. doing duty in his /P/S collected on H.D horses from HQ "A" "B" & "C" Bde + one from 38 Brig as pr instructions from D.A.D.R A.D.V.S. issued draft instructions to send gun chgrs of N.S.Y. & FRUGES. Recd 5 horses from "B" Sqn N.S.Y.	
	29/4/16		Capt Johnston called. Recd two horses from N.S.Y. two from 6M. B Sqn and 10 NCO + m inoculated. H.H.& one to A D V S at FRUGES H.H.&	
	30/4/16		R.H.A. Grey Chgr of N.S.Y. sent to A D V S at FRUGES H.H.&	

WAR DIARY
or
INTELLIGENCE SUMMARY

Army Form C. 2118

Place	Date	Hour	Summary of Events and Information	Remarks and references to Appendices
LEBIEZ	1/5/16		Recd. 3 horses from 1st Royals (Chargers) and 2 from N.&Y. Cav. Sergt Stephens & two men proceeded to FAQUENBERGUES with 3 AD horses handed them over to 3rd Reserve Park No SR 11 Rpt Wilson by J. B granted 6 days leave to England. JRS	
	2/5/16		Recd one horse from 1st Royals + one from 3rd Bde R.B. A.D.V.S. ordered Section to hand over 2 horses to Harwood. JRS	
	3/5/16		Recd one horse from Maj Cox Ba. Evacuated 8 horses to NEUFCHATEL JRS	
	4/5/16		Recd one horse from 6th Royal. 1 noot injured through kicking. JRS	
	5/5/16		Recd one Chgr from Royals took horse from Aux H.T. Coy. ballotted one chgr from Maj' ARMITAGE GHQ Staff at NEUVILLE in accordance with instructions recvd by DADR. JRS	
	6/5/16		Ballotted 1 Chgr from C.Batty R.H.A. JRS	
	7/5/16		Sergt Stephens tomhani to FOND-DE-MOURIEZ to deliver charger to Light Trench Mortar School. Pte Tendale proceeded on leave to England. Capt Bellison returned from leave. JRS	
	8/5/16		Visited 3rd Bde Stat one and horses. Returns met. One Chgr sent Reg. also by order of D.A.D.R. JRS	

WAR DIARY
or
INTELLIGENCE SUMMARY.
(Erase heading not required.)

Army Form C. 2118.

Place	Date	Hour	Summary of Events and Information	Remarks and references to Appendices
	9/5/16		A.D.V.S. visited Section inspected horses + ordered 12 horses to be evacuated including Major ERSKIN'S Chgr. "C"Bat.RHA JRS	
	10/5/16		Visited "C" Batty. + 3DG JRS	
	11/5/16		Evacuated 4 sick + 3 cast horses to ABBEVILLE + 8 sick to NEUFCHATEL JRS	
	12/5/16		Inspected horses of 3 DG's + some of "C" Batty RHA. Took over 2 horses from "C" Batty JRS A.D.V.S. + D.A.D.R. visited Section + ordered the horses to be sent to Royals which were cast this day, + one to be sent to HUCQUELIERS tomorrow at noon. Recvd. one from Royals. Collected one H.D. horse from 1/1 Yorks Bgd. from Rest Camp. New PRESSIN. JRS	
	13/5/16		Recvd orders to march to training ground at ST. RIQUIER. Dept. 6 horses to No 20 M.V.S. by order of A.D.V.S. JRS. Recvd. one horse from "O" Batty R.H.A JRS	
	14/5/16		Inspected horses of Roeselen. JRS	

WAR DIARY
or
INTELLIGENCE SUMMARY
(Erase heading not required.)

Army Form C. 2118

Instructions regarding War Diaries and Intelligence Summaries are contained in F.S. Regs., Part II. and the Staff Manual respectively. Title Pages will be prepared in manuscript.

Place	Date	Hour	Summary of Events and Information	Remarks and references to Appendices
REBIEZ	15/5/16	4 AM	Reveille	Ref. KR N°s — ABBEVILLE Sheets 1/100,000
		4-6AM	Watered fed stables breakfast	
		6:25	Moved off	
		7:10	Arrived at rendezvous attached rendez at Bq of BEAURAINVILLE	
		7:30	Moved off. Order of march: Peloton HQ, 6th Bn Typal Troop; 3rd Bn; Royals; "C" Batty RHA; 5th Car Bd Amb N°13 H.V.S.	
			Route the X roads just W of BEAURAIN CHATEAU — MARESQUEL — CHANDAG—aux—BOIS — LAMBUS —TURTEFONTAINE — CRECY — DONVAST — STRIQUER	
			Raining very heavily until 10:30 AM.	
DOMPIERRE		11 AM	Watered fed, watering facilities prod. running stream of good water	
		11:45 AM	Moved arrived at	
STRIQUER		PM 3:15	Horses picketed in open, men billeted in town.	
		3:30	Watered + stables	
		4:15	fnd. Good watering place running stream. Visited "C" Batty RHA	
			Wired A.D.V.S. Sit of casualties	
	16/5/16	5:30 AM	Reveille	
		6:00-7	Watering exercise	
			Watered fed	
		7-7:20	Breakfast	
		7:45-9		
		8 AM	Sick parade Bds HQ 8m + 6th Car Bd Amb. though no casualties	
		10 AM	Visited 3 DG. with Capt NICHOLSON afternoon visited C Batty	
		10:30 AM	Watered	
		10 PM	exercise	
		12:15 PM	watered + fed	
		2:30 PM	watered	
		4-5	Stables watered fed	
		8.0	Hayed up	
		6	Wired info list of casualties to A.D.V.S. having visited units under my charge. Very warm day no rain.	Very warm day. Roads in good order

WAR DIARY or INTELLIGENCE SUMMARY

Army Form C. 2118

(Erase heading not required.)

Instructions regarding War Diaries and Intelligence Summaries are contained in F.S. Regs., Part II. and the Staff Manual respectively. Title Pages will be prepared in manuscript.

Place	Date	Hour	Summary of Events and Information	Remarks and references to Appendices
ST RIQUIER	17/5/16	5:30 AM	Reveille	LENS — A 33B VILLE Sheet 1/100,000
		6–8 AM	Widely exercise	
		8–8:30	Watered fed	
		8:30–9:15	Breakfast	
		9:15 AM	Stables	
		8:30 AM	Limber Brakes hitched tat back.	
		10 AM	Watered. Winter 'C' Batty R.H.A	
		11 AM	Winter 3/DG Capt Nicholson took over temp/c	
		12:15 PM	Watered fed. A.D.V.S. arrived	
		2 PM	Reco'd details came from 6th G Sqn.	
		2:30 PM	Watered. Winter 'C' Batty R.H.A	
		4 PM	Took over a horse from unit a mare cast belongs to 1st Batt R.9 Fus & this suffered from acute pneumonia. Found a necessity. However in charge returned to his regiment attached another horse.	
		4:45	Winter 2 bds who had 13 convalescent. 'C' Batty R.H.A 1, Bde Hdqrs + Co Fed & nil.	
		4:30	Watered fed	
		6 PM	Winter A.D.V.S list of casualties	
		6:30 PM	Horse recd from R 9 Fus died.	
		8 PM	Horse up received orders to Rendezvous at 4:30 AM tomorrow. Very warm day no rain.	
	18/5/16	4 AM	Reveille	
		4:5:30	Watered fed stables breakfast	
		5:35 AM	Moved off to rendezvous X road 1200 yds S.S.E. of YVRENCH, at 4:30 proceeded to HEIRMONT thence L BERNATRE being midway between MAIZICOURT & MONTIGNY at 9.50 AM.	
		10:35 AM	Moved to CONTEVILLE via MONTIGNY — AGENVILLE — DOMLEGER	
		12 NOON	Fed	
		1:30 PM	Watered	
		3:30 PM	Left CONTEVILLE returned to ST RIQUIER via ONEUX arriving about 4:20 PM.	
		4:20 PM	Watered fed	

WAR DIARY
or
INTELLIGENCE SUMMARY
(Erase heading not required.)

Army Form C. 2118

Instructions regarding War Diaries and Intelligence Summaries are contained in F. S. Regs., Part II. and the Staff Manual respectively. Title Pages will be prepared in manuscript.

Place	Date	Hour	Summary of Events and Information	Remarks and references to Appendices
ST RIQUIER	18/5/16	5·PM	Visited 'C' Batty R.H.A. 6th Cav to lunt; Bde HdQrs; made interesting returns. Recvd. two horses from Remts. for evacuation. Recvd. notice from Bde Hd'q Boladin + No 13 DVS would not parade tomorrow	Ref LENS - ABBEVILLE 1/100,000
		6·5PM	Wired ADVS list of casualties. Warm day no rain. JRS	
	19/5/16	6·0AM	Reveille	
		8 AM	Routine. Visited 'C' Batty R.H.A. Bde HQ + 6th Cav to lunt. rejoin in the afternoon on their return	
		5 AM	Recvd. two horses from Remt Vet offrs from 12hr	
		6·15PM	Wired ADVS Casualty list. Very Warm no rain. JRS	
	20/5/16	6·0AM	Reveille Routine	
		8 AM	Visited units under my charge	
		9·30AM	Recvd. one horse for Remts. (Sgt Tindale OM)	
		11·50AM	Wired A.D.V.S. rest evacuation of horses	
		3PM	Evacuated 9 horses GABBEVILLE.	
		6·15PM	Wired Casualty list to ADVS. JRS	
		9·0PM	Recvd. orders from Bde HQ, ref. Return to billets at LEBIEZ. Very warm day no rain.	
	21/5/16	6AM	Recvd. one horse from NSY (Private Muir) (11 mls)	
		9·10AM	Started from Rendezvous attached roads due S. of S. in ARGENVILLERS. I was put in charge of Bde Hdqr. led horses transport. Route from DOMVAST - LABROYE - HESDIN - LALOGE - LEBIEZ	
LE BOISLE		11·40AM	Watered & fed	
CAVRON - ST. MARTIN		12·15PM	Moved off	
		3·25PM	Watered	

Army Form C. 2118

WAR DIARY
or
INTELLIGENCE SUMMARY
(Erase heading not required.)

Instructions regarding War Diaries and Intelligence Summaries are contained in F. S. Regs., Part II. and the Staff Manual respectively. Title Pages will be prepared in manuscript.

Place	Date	Hour	Summary of Events and Information	Remarks and references to Appendices
LEBIEZ	21/5/16	4.45 PM	Arrived in old billets	
		5.0 PM	Water fed stables afterwards at 6 PM. Warm day no rain.	
			Shoes did not wear well, roads in good order.	

WAR DIARY
or
INTELLIGENCE SUMMARY

Army Form C. 2118

(Erase heading not required.)

Place	Date	Hour	Summary of Events and Information	Remarks and references to Appendices
KEBIEZ	22/5/16		Routine visit to Bde Hd Qrs. JRS	
	23/5/16		Rec'd five horses from 3 Bde, one from N.S.Yeo + one from 6th M.G. Sqn. also three from 1st Royals, returned one to N.S.Y. A.D.V.S. visited section JRS	
	24/5/16		Evacuated 12 horses to Neufchatel. JRS	
	25/5/16		Saddlery inspection JRS	
	26/5/16		Visited A.D.V.S. at Fruges with returns forward JRS	
	27/5/16		Rec'd wire from D.A.D.R. to collect horse of Capt WAVELL from NEUVILLE on 29/5/16 JRS	
	28/5/16		Inspected horses of Bde Hd Qrs. JRS	
	29/5/16		Rec'd 11 horses for Remounts (one for treatment) collected horse from NEUVILLE. Rifle drill. Rec'd. one horse from 3 Fd. Sqn RE + two from 3rd Cy Sqn RE JRS	
	30/5/16		Rec'd 3 horses to N.S.Y. (one for treatment) Kit inspection. Visited sick of Ration Qrs. JRS	
	31/5/16		Rec'd two horses from R. Flying Corps, one from "L" Battery. gone from N.S.Y. for transpt. Evacuated 16 horses to NEUFCHATEL. Received horse from Lt. Col. DILLON at NEUVILLE. JRS	

Army Form C. 2118.

WAR DIARY
or
INTELLIGENCE SUMMARY.
(Erase heading not required.)

Instructions regarding War Diaries and Intelligence Summaries are contained in F. S. Regs., Part II. and the Staff Manual respectively. Title pages will be prepared in manuscript.

Place	Date	Hour	Summary of Events and Information	Remarks and references to Appendices
LE BIEZ	1/6/		Visited Bde. Hd. Qrs. Made out Weekly Returns. Aiming Drill. Returned 1 horse to N.S.Y. cured.	
	2/6/		Received 1 horse from C. Squadron N.S.Y. for treatment & one charger from Bde. Hd. Qrs. for transfer to 4th D. Gds. by order of D.A.D.R. Brought 1 horse to Col. HERRICK, A.D.M.S. 3rd C.D. JRD	
	3/6/		Received 2 horses from G Batty R.H.A. & 3 from C Batty R.H.A. 2 from N.S.Y. 1 from Captain Fielding, Hd. Qrs. 3 C.D. & 1 from Royals for treatment. Sent horse to Captain Fielding collected from Captain Wavell at NEUVILL on 28/5/16 & 1 received for transfer from N.S.Y. on 31/5/16 sent to Royals. 2 horses returned cured to N.S.Y. JRD	
	4/6/		Inspected horses of Bde. Hd. Qrs. Sent 1 L.D. to 9th Cav. Fd. Amb. & 1 horse of Royal Sco sent to BRIXNET to Reserve Park. JRD	
	5/6/		Received 6 horses from Royals (3 of which went for treatment), 2 from N.S.Y. & 4 from G Batty R.H.A. Handed over one horse to A.D.V.S. Collected horse of 1st Life Gds. from Mile DOLLE at SAINS-Les-FRESSIN left by M.M.V.S. SE 14431 Pte. Phillips, D.W. reported for duty by order of A.D.V.S. JRD	

2353 Wt. W3544/1454 700,000 5/15 D. D. & L. A.D.S.S./Forms/C 2118.

WAR DIARY or INTELLIGENCE SUMMARY.

Army Form C. 2118.

Place	Date	Hour	Summary of Events and Information	Remarks and references to Appendices
LEBIEZ	6/9/16		Sent Sergt. & 5 men to BEAURAINVILLE for Remounts. They brought back one horse for Col. Cummins A.S.C. 3C.D. which was taken over same evening. Received 2 Debility cases from 4th Bde. R.H.A. Ammunition Column.	JRS
	7/9/16		ADVS called & inspected sick horses. Evacuated 19 to NEUFCHATEL. Received 1 from 6th Field Squadron. Visited C Batty R.H.A.	JRS
	8/9/16		Returned one Debility case to 4th Bde R.H.A Amm. Col. by order of ADVS. Sent horse ex Regale to Aug. H.T. Coy. FRUGES by order of DADR. Received horse from Captain Fielding as unfit for charger Rover. Destroyed one horse of g Batty received on 3/6/16 and found Near Bone diseased & chronic in gastrocnemius. Made out Weekly Returns. Visited C Batty R.H.A. His Inspection.	JRS
	9/9/16		Received charger of Major General Campbell's for treatment for Splint O.F. Rifle Drill. Visited C Batty.	JRS
	10/9/16		Received 2 horses from C Batty R.H.A. & 2 from N.S.Y. for treatment. Visited C Batty.	
	11/9/16		Inspected horses of Bde Hd Qrs. & destroyed horse of N.S.Y. which had fallen & broken its knees.	JRS

WAR DIARY or INTELLIGENCE SUMMARY

Army Form C. 2118

Place	Date	Hour	Summary of Events and Information	Remarks and references to Appendices
LE BIEZ	12/6/16		Recd. 1 horse from 3rd D.G. for treatment (strain); two from 6th M G Sqdn, 3 from 1st Royals. Visited 3rd Bde vet N.S.Y.	
	13/6/16		Inspected changed units by Lieut Campbell, to O.C. 1st Bde byorder of A.A.D.R. Recd 3 horses from 1st Royals. A.D.V.S. called, inspected unit horses for evacuation. Transferred charges out in Cpt visiting to integrate 6 Cav. Bde.	
	14/6/16		Recd two cast horses from 6th Signal Troop, evacuated 1 unit to ABBEVILLE. Visited 3rd Bde M G Sqdn + 6th 'B' Batty R.H.A.	
	15/6/16		Recd 1 horse from N.S.Y. Visited 'D' Batty + M G Sqdn 2 Bde 15th Cav Fd Amb.	
	16/6/16		Recd from 'C' Batty R.H.A. horse (attached Aux.H.T.Co) for treatment & another from the Battery for evacuation. Visited 3rd Bde & 1st M G Sqdn.	
	17/6/16		Inspected B. Sqn. N.S.Y. visited sick of 'C' Batty RHA & 1st M G Sqdn + N.S.Y.(A+C) M2.	
	18/6/16		Inspected horses of HdQrs 6th Cav Bde + C Sqdn N.S.Y. N. SF 692 Pt. SIMMONDS A. Dispatched to No 2 Vety Hpl ROUEN in accordance with instruction received from A.D.V.S. Recd orders to return to move shortly.	
	19/6/16		Attended G.O.C's Inspection of horses 1st Recd 4 horses from N.S.Y. & from P.KEEN.E. sent to Hpl with influenza. Recd. 4 horses from N.S.Y. & from 3rdD.G. 2 horses of M G Sqn. Visited A.D.V.S. at FRUGES. G.O.C. 6 C.B. visited Sqdn 3rd DR. Recd from 15th & 16th Cavalier 3ED	
	20/6/16		M.I. removed from MONTREUIL with Sergt + 3/m. A.D.V.S. came on to inspect transfer sick horses. Recd 1 from N.S.Y. troubomma 1 to N.S.Y. visited sick of N.S.Y.	

WAR DIARY or INTELLIGENCE SUMMARY

Army Form C. 2118.

Place	Date	Hour	Summary of Events and Information	Remarks and references to Appendices
LE BIEZ	21/6/16		Promenade & pick nut leave ABBEVILLE, recd. for 1/sect for "C" Batty RHA + one civ from 3 Sqn R.B. also two from N.S.Y. Sent (without woman despatched to ANNIN to collect one mule left by 14 D.A.C. by order of A.D.V.S. Saddler to inspection. Returned two horses to "C" Batty RHA (1 arm H.T. Cry attached) which had been sent in for treatment.	
	22/6/16		Recd 4 horses from 3 Bde two from Ravyr + 1 Chgr from b M.G Sqdn in exchange for 1 horse of "C" Batty (had it yesterday in cart) by order of ADR A.D.V.S. Indeaerate + inspected horse Victoria rest of Pinckstel. "C" Batty 16"Cos 3d Bde made out return unebower Cb0 exit from 3 Bde sent to Cas Hd Ud (1 replace Veminibs spare sent in by them on 19/6/16) by raw of ADR.	
	23/6/16		Recd 1 Chgr from Claim Office 3 Cb as under. Thirteen from 3 Sqdqn R.E., three from N.S.Y., one chgr from Maj Gen J. Vaughan C.B. & 90 to be vaccinated for breeding purposes. Recd 6 from b M.G. Sqdn.	
	24/6/16		Recd 9 for evacuation from 20 M.V.S. Dental M.C. Sgdshene to Regals for duty to another "C" Batty RHA (cast on 21/6) to the Royals also by order A.D.R. Allocating two from 3 Bde at BEAURAINVILLE & vaccinated 45 horses + 1 mule to MBREVILLE.	

WAR DIARY or INTELLIGENCE SUMMARY

Army Form C. 2118.

(Erase heading not required.)

Instructions regarding War Diaries and Intelligence Summaries are contained in F. S. Regs., Part II. and the Staff Manual respectively. Title pages will be prepared in manuscript.

Place	Date	Hour	Summary of Events and Information	Remarks and references to Appendices
	24/6/16	6.30 PM	Left LE BIEZ at 6.30 + rendezvous'd at T Road due E. of Pt. of St VAAST at 9.15 PM + went via HESDIN - RE GNAVILLE - LABROYE - + arrived at DOMVAST at 3:30 AM on 25/6/16. Billeted in Bivouac horses in open. F	ABBEVILLE 1/100000
DOMVAST	25/6/16		Visited S'Batty. and HdQrs of Bde. met Bde. V.O's at 1. P.M.	
	26/6/16		4th N. of X in YVRENCHEUX traversed thro DOMQUEUR - DOMART - camped at ST LEGER - En - DOMART at 2.45 AM on 2-6 inst. Before moving off Meade's horse from M.I. 6th C. 2nd Aust. which is brought along with us. A.V.V.S. within section at 10.24 AM.	
ST LEGER En - DOMART	"	8.15 PM	Visited C Batty R.H.A. Rode thro' front trees V Doapelle. LEFT ST. LEGER + marched via VIGNACOURT - BERTANGLES - COISY - ALLONVILLE - QUERRIEU - BONNAY. Harness + turnouts of some men an eyesore.	
	27/6/16		Trained at Harness at 5 AM on 27th. Horses grazed in open near an inn/Shower.	
	28/6/16		Heavy rain storms from Royals + 1 from N.S.W.	
	29/6/16		Horses from N.S.W. much worse than from A.V.V.S. Evacuated 6 N.S.W. M.X.9. brought the Shoein horses one which had ulcerated at two near from S.D.G. which had in the needs Told D.	
			Packed all transport ready to leave off. Harrow. I have the 6th H.G. Spht + H.m Royals, Indian Black and C. Batt M'C Adella mancart with liner. And made special from A.V.S, + other section am	
			Distinguish in drawing supplies from S.D. for Troops.	

Army Form C. 2118.

WAR DIARY
or
INTELLIGENCE SUMMARY.

(Erase heading not required.)

Place	Date	Hour	Summary of Events and Information	Remarks and references to Appendices
BONNAY	30/10		Received 2 horse from 20th. Hrs. Front/Att Pro (amp) which came up on a tramand last night Had order to evacuate all sick to No. 20 H.S. Evacuated 9 to 20 H.S. JPS	

WAR DIARY or INTELLIGENCE SUMMARY

Army Form C. 2118

13th M.V.S.

Vol 78

Place	Date	Hour	Summary of Events and Information	Remarks and references to Appendices
BONNAY	1/7/16	8AM / 5PM	Roads ordered to addles up at 9AM, unsaddled at 8AM returned to stand to at ½ hours notice. Drew rations + stand to at 2 hours. JRJ	
"	2/7/16	5AM	Bath. received visited "C" Batty R.H.A. & Buckleps. JRJ	
"	3/7/16	6:30	Re horses. Hotross 1 horse from 6th M.G. Sqdn. Read instruction to pack &c. JRJ	
			Re harness. Hotress Times at 5 AM on hind. Evacuated one horse to 20 MVS under our instructions from A.D.V.S. Drew for 500 w.t. Cashier. JRJ	
"	4/7/16	3AM	Recd. Move offset 5:50AM & arrived at MERELESSART at 6PM. Horses then under corn. JRJ	
			A.D.V.S. visited section. Privates "C" Batty R.H.A. & 8th Cav Bde Cav Bde. JRJ	
MERELESSART	5/7/16		Read. visited section. Privates "C" Batty R.H.A. & 8th Cav Bde. JRJ	
"	6/7/16		Recd. 1 horse for help "3" C Div. Read orders for Bde transport the ready to move at 1½ hrs notice from 6AM 7 inst. Hotress four horses from 6th M.G.Sqdn. 1 from N.S.Y 1 from Royals. & 6 from 3rd B.P. JRJ	
"	7/7/16	2:30AM / 8AM	Read orders for Railhead at LONGPRE evacuated 17 horses to FORGES-LES-FAUX returned then to MERELESSART. Stood to until 9 PM when orders was cancelled. JRJ	
"	8/7/16		Orders to prepare to move at 1 PM. at which hour we marched to CORBIE arrived at 4:30AM on 9/7/16. JRJ	

WAR DIARY
or
INTELLIGENCE SUMMARY.
(Erase heading not required.)

Army Form C. 2118.

Place	Date	Hour	Summary of Events and Information	Remarks and references to Appendices
CORBIE	9/7/16	AM 4.30	Horses taken in open. ADVS inspected Section. Rec'd orders at 4.15 PM to be ready to move at 6.35 PM to New area. JRJ	
		PM 6.35	Moved off to VAUX and arrived at 9.30 PM. Horses watered in open. JRJ	
VAUX	10/7/16		Rec'd 3 horses from 6 M.G. Sqn, 3 from Royals 3 from N.S.Y. & 9 from 32 D.G. JRJ	
	11/7/16		Rec'd one horse from N.S.Y. JRJ	
	12/7/16		Took on inshoe from the Qr. 6 C.B. Evacuated 18 horses No.12 Mob. Vety. Section supplied the conducting party. ADVS inspected section. Inspected Gastelnest. JRJ	
	13/7/16		Took out one horse from 6th Tu Rile M.G.Sqn, 5 from Royals, 1 from 6 M.G. Sqn., + 1 from N.S.Y. Evacuated 7 horses. Rec'd orders to stand to from 4 AM to 14th inst. JRJ	
	14/7/16		Rev. at 2 AM. saddled up paraded at 4 AM, unsaddled & stood to at 5 hrs notice to move. JRJ	
	15/7/16		Rev at 3.30 AM to stand to ready to move at 5 hrs notice. Rec'd 1 horse from Royals. JRJ	
	16/7/16		Rev. at 5 AM. Rec'd two horses from 3 D.G., four from 6 M.G. Sqdn. one from N.S.Y. Sent to vet. Evacuated 8 + N 20 M.V.S. Got on 30th. JRJ	128
	17/7/16		Rec'd 4 from Royals one of which was a fractured wrist & had to move. Rec'd orders to form 8 PM at 2 hrs notice. JRJ	
	18/7/16		Routine. JRJ	
	19/7/16		Rev'd at 5.30 AM. Rec'd orders to be ready to move off at 5.35 PM. saddled up at 3 PM. moved to	

WAR DIARY or INTELLIGENCE SUMMARY

Army Form C. 2118.

Place	Date	Hour	Summary of Events and Information	Remarks and references to Appendices
LA NEUVILLE	19/7/16		rendezvous at 3.30 pm & marched to LA NEUVILLE arriving at 5:45 PM. Horses in open. JR?	
	20/7/16		A.D.V.S. visited station. Returned one horse to Remts. Recd 4 from N.S.Y. & 4 from 3rd D.G. JR?	
	21/7/16		Recd 3 from 1st Royals & 1 from 6th M.G. Sqdn. Evacuated 11 to FORGES-LES-EAUX. Returned charger of Maj. Gen. Campbell wnd. JR?	
	22/7/16		Saddle inspection & Routine. JR?	
	23/7/16		Rifle Inspection routine. JR?	
	24/7/16		Received 4 from Royals & 4 from N.S.Y. JR?	
	25/7/16		Evacuated 9 horses to FORGES-LES-EAUX. JR?	
	26/7/16		A.D.V.S. visited section & examined supply of Cordite/Casualty party from our section. No S.E. 982 PHILADE T.E. evacuated to Hospital with ravines vein. Medical Inspection of whole section. JR?	
	27/7/16		A.D.V.S. visited Section. JR?	
	28/7/16		Recd six horses from Royals & 1 from C Batty, R.H.A. took over two from No 20 N.S. belong to 8th M.G. Sqdn. Left Holland, C taken over by 6th Cav. Fd Amb. by tractor/Fofoculis. Pte Kennmore evacuated to 14th field ambc suffering from diabetes mismanaged. JR?	
	29/7/16	AM 5:30	Rev. morning exercise, four mile. Sent to No 6 Cav Fd Amb. for evacuation Medical Inspection of whole Section. A.D.V.S. visited section. JR?	

Army Form C. 2118.

WAR DIARY
or
INTELLIGENCE SUMMARY.
(Erase heading not required.)

Instructions regarding War Diaries and Intelligence Summaries are contained in F. S. Regs., Part II. and the Staff Manual respectively. Title pages will be prepared in manuscript.

Place	Date	Hour	Summary of Events and Information	Remarks and references to Appendices
KANEUVILLE	30/7/16		Routine NDR	
	31/7/16		Rec'd two horses from N.&V. 1 from Bungalo 1 from 3rd S.H. transferred them to FORGES-LES-EAUX for No. 12 M.V.S. Rec'd orders the ready to move at 6 AM on 1-8-16. ARW.C.	
			in ½ a Section. JR)	

T2134. Wt. W708—776. 500000. 4/15. Sir J. C. & S.

Army Form C. 2118.

WAR DIARY
or
INTELLIGENCE SUMMARY.
(Erase heading not required.)

Place	Date	Hour	Summary of Events and Information	Remarks and references to Appendices
LA NEUVILLE	1/8/16	6 AM	Moved off & marched to LE HESGE arriving at 3.30 PM. Horse picketed in empty barns. Received orders to move at 5 AM on 2nd inst. A.D.V.S. visited section. Cpl Hubbard returned from M.C. Sanita Anal. JRS	
	2/8/16	2.30 AM	Rev. moved off at 5 AM marched to L'HEURE arriving at 3 PM. Billeted attachments, horses in yard, men bivouaced in field. JRS	
	3/8/16		Recd. 9 horses from 3 D.G. 3 from N.S.Y. 4 from 7th Royals. A.D.V.S. visited section in forenoon. Evacuated 15 horses to No. 2.2 Vety Hpl. ABBEVILLE by road. Recd. orders the ready horses at 4.15 AM that Sergt. Lukehurst TG taken over for treatment (Diarhea) by No. 6 Cav Field Amb. JRS	
	4/8/16	11.30 AM	Rev. moved off at 4.15 AM marched to MAINTENAY arriving at 11.30 AM horses & men bivouaced in orchard. JRS	
	5/8/16 6/8/16	5 AM	Rev. moved off at 4 AM marched to LEBIEZ into stabillite. JRS Collected horses left by Royals at MAINTENAY & MAYOR refused to accept anything for keep of same & wd. not take horses down from No. 2 made arrangements to take over the two horses left by 3 I.G. at ROUSSENT, as unable to move.	
	7/8/16		One Cpl. & 7 Men went to GOUY-ST-ANDRE & BUIRE-LES-SEC, & obtained two fresh	

WAR DIARY or INTELLIGENCE SUMMARY

Army Form C. 2118.

Place	Date	Hour	Summary of Events and Information	Remarks and references to Appendices
NEBIEZ	7/8/16		+ took over the horses of 3 Dg. Took over 4 horses from Royals, & two from 6th H.Q. Sqdn. No. SE 4704 Pte JAMES I.T. reported for duty from No 7 VetHosp FORGES-LES-EAUX. proceeded to 1000 from FdAmbul. /RJ	
	8/8/16		Took over onehorse from N.S.Y. + 4 from 3 DG. ADVS visited section inspected horses + vaccination /RJ	
	9/8/16		Evacuated 16 horses to NEUFCHATEL, have collected from ROUSSENT belong to 3DG, were taken over by Regt. as it had improved rapidly. SE 3613 Pte Lawrence J reported to duty from No 39 General Hospital Rifle inspection. Received 3 cart horses from "Royals	
	10/8/16			
	11/8/16			
	12/8/16		Movement train at BEAUVAIN VILLE with NCO + 5 men. Sergt Hutchins of 2/g reported for duty from No 6 Conv Ct. Ambul. after treatment for diarrhoea.	
	13/8/16		Inspected Saddlery & Gas Helmets.	
	14/8/16		Took over 4 horses from Royals + two 6th H. Gun Sqdn. + also 3 for treatment from N.S.Y. Two from No 6 Cav Fd Ambl.	
	15/8/16		Received 4 horses from 3rd Fd Sqadn R.E. 1 from N.S.Y. + 4 from 3DG No 6457 Pte HILL G.W. reported to duty from No 4 Vet Hosp FORGES-LES-EAUX	

Army Form C. 2118.

WAR DIARY
or
INTELLIGENCE SUMMARY.
(Erase heading not required.)

Instructions regarding War Diaries and Intelligence Summaries are contained in F. S. Regs., Part II. and the Staff Manual respectively. Title pages will be prepared in manuscript.

Place	Date	Hour	Summary of Events and Information	Remarks and references to Appendices
LEBIEZ	16/8/16		A.D.V.S. visited Section inspected horses for evacuation JRJ	
	17/8/16		Evacuated 23 sick & 4 cast horses to No 2 Vety Hpl ABBEVILLE JRJ	
	18/8/16		Took over 1 horse from N.S.Y. for treatment. SE6023 Pte WEED S.M. sent to No.	
	19/8/16		2 Vety Hpl HAVRE being surplus Establishment. JRJ	
			Took over 1 horse from HQrs N.S.Y. No.608 Sergt STEPHENS.F.G. SE3613 Pte LAWRENCE	
			G. & Dr. CHAMBERLAIN.A. A.S.C. ex-attached for dental treatment returned same day JRJ	
	19/8/16		Routine. JRJ	
	20/8/16		Routine JRJ	
	21/8/16		No horses to have transferred and 3 from N.S.Y. JRJ	
	22/8/16		Recd. one horse from 3rd H. Bgde. R.F.A. 2 from H. Fdr. Amb. Col., also one from N.S.Y. A.S.V.8 under Section inspected horses JRJ	
	23/8/16		Evacuated 16 sick took one one to N.S.Y. for treatment one for evacuation Returned	
			one to N.S.Y. card of skin disease JRJ	
	24/8/16		Recd. one horse from Royals, one from 4th Bde R.H.A. Hqrs. JRJ	
	25/8/16		All day cattle parade at ROYON. JRJ	
	26/8/16		Rifle firing practice JRJ	

WAR DIARY
or
INTELLIGENCE SUMMARY.
(Erase heading not required.)

Army Form C. 2118.

Place	Date	Hour	Summary of Events and Information	Remarks and references to Appendices
LEBIEZ	27/6		Took over one horse from HdQrs 3 box. Sir M.M.P. att. in by A.D.V.S. with Mag. Whitehands. JRS	
	28/6		Took over three horses from "C" Batty R.H.A. two from Royals one from M.M.P. 6th Coy Ride for treatment. Drew h. 1000, from the banker JRS	
	29/6		Recvd. two horses from 4th Bed Amn. hd R.H.A. one from 81st Coy A.S.C. one from 7 Bde. Rifle Shortly JRS.	
	30/6		Evacuated 12 sick. one cas. to ABBEVILLE JRS	
	31/6		Recvd. 4 cast horses from Royals for two evacuation JRS.	

WAR DIARY or INTELLIGENCE SUMMARY

Army Form C. 2118.

Place	Date	Hour	Summary of Events and Information	Remarks and references to Appendices
LEBIEZ	1/9/16		ROUTINE JRB	
	2/9/16		Attended G.O.C's inspection of No 6 Coy Fd Amb. Rifle firing practice JRB	
	3/9/16		S.E. 93+4 Pte Parcon R.T. proceeded on 7 days leave to England. JRB	
	4/9/16		Recd nine horses (7 cart + 2 vetry cases) from 3 D.B., two hired horses of M.M.P 6 C.B. JRB	
	5/9/16		" two horses & Col Womells Chgr from 'A' Royals. A.D.V.S. visited section +	
			inspected sick horse for inoculation. A.D.V.S. took out one of the horses sent in by Royals today JRB	
	6/9/16		Recd one colt horse from 'C' Batty R.H.A. Evacuated 23 horses to ABBEVILLE	
	7/9/16		D.D.V.S (Col O'mon Conaghan) visited Section with A.D.V.S. JRB	
	8/9/16		Recd nine horses from 'A' Royals + three from 3 D.B.s also five from No 14 M.V.S. JRB	
	9/9/16		Recd one horse from 'Y' Cav Fd Amb. & No 14 M.V.S. Two for 'C' Batty R.H.A. one from	
			3 DB's & two from N.C.Y. Evacuated 19 sick + 4 cast to ABBEVILLE	
			Ordered to be ready to move tomorrow. Returned one horse A116 to N.S.Y. evnd JRB	
	10/9/16		Left LEBIEZ at 8.45 AM arrived at DOMINOIS at 1 PM. Took over 1 horse from N.S.Y. A116 (Runt foot) Brown	
			4yr 500 oz Fd Indian. JRB	
	11/9/16		Left DOMINOIS at 2.10 PM and arrived at DRUCAT at 6 PM JRB	
	12/9/16		Left DRUCAT and arrived at oa CHAUSSÉE TIRANCOURT about 5 PM in centeau formades JRB	

Army Form C. 2118.

WAR DIARY
or
INTELLIGENCE SUMMARY.
(Erase heading not required.)

Instructions regarding War Diaries and Intelligence Summaries are contained in F. S. Regs., Part II. and the Staff Manual respectively. Title pages will be prepared in manuscript.

Place	Date	Hour	Summary of Events and Information	Remarks and references to Appendices
LA CHAUSSÉE TIRANCOURT	13/9/16		Evacuated 14 horses from HANGEST to No.1 V.H. PICQUIGNY-LES-EAUX. Rode to harness from 3rd Fd. Sqdn. R.E. JRS	
	14/9/16		Left TIRANCOURT at 9:30 AM & proceeded to BUSSY-LES-DOURS arriving at 4 P.M. Road 1 horse from 60th Bn. Cyclists. Drew horse Ration for tradays. JRS	
	15/9/16		Left Bussy to accompanies R.Rd. to S.W. of BONNAY. Met Capt. HARDING AVS oc. No 14/VS who said A.D.V.S. had given him orders to proceed to LANEUVILLE & inform me. A.D.V.S. arrived at Section & came with me to LANEUVILLE. The three actions being in bivouac together. Division to JRS	
LANEUVILLE	16/9/16		Visited R.Rs. rec'd 15 B. Battalions for evacuation. Rec'd 1 from O'Battery 1 from N.S.Y. + 2 from 3 DG JRS	
	17/9/16	6 AM	Ordered to move to PONT NOYELLES at 7:30 AM, with 14 H.V.S.	
		7 AM	Handed over 4 horses to 20 H.V.S. which was awaiting orders & at 9:30 proceeded to PONT NOYELLES where we joined our Ration JRS	
PONT NOYELLES	18/9/16		Visited units under my charge & went details to officers to find out re Protoculation	
	19/9/16		Took over to horses from Rayal 3 from N.S.Y. Rifle inspection. A.D.V.S. visited Section. Rec'd 1 sick + 3 castration from N. Irish Horse	
	20/9/16		Took over 1 horse from 14th Section Rutasjy & 1 left 4th yrs. Evacuation 9 sick + 3 cast from FRECHENCOURT for conducting parties from 20 N.V.S. to N° 7 V.H. FORGES-LES-EAUX. JRS	

T2134. Wt. W708—776. 500000. 4/15. Sir J. C. & S.

WAR DIARY
or
INTELLIGENCE SUMMARY.
(Erase heading not required.)

Army Form C. 2118.

Instructions regarding War Diaries and Intelligence Summaries are contained in F.S. Regs., Part II. and the Staff Manual respectively. Title pages will be prepared in manuscript.

Place	Date	Hour	Summary of Events and Information	Remarks and references to Appendices
PONT NOYELLES	21/9/16		No 6475 Pte HILL G.W. Ave admitted 47 F.Am with "Synovitis knee" SE11659 Pte Jones A. reported sick. Defective Vision. but was attended Casuals. Read/Lowe from N.S.Y. 3 from 3 BSe. new arrangements with O.C. M.20. M.V.S. terminated our lease previously paid. New Scheme to Heb Section Read. orders to be ready forward by 12 noon tomorrow. JRS	
	22/9/16		Moved off at 12 noon transferred to SOUES ordin. turned in at HQ farm house in LEMEIGE	LEMEIGE OUES
SOUES	23/9/16		Took over 1 house from Royd + N.O. informed me he was leaving 3 houses in town in SOUES which could not well move off at 9 AM moved at WAVANS JRS	
SAULCHOY	24/9/16	6 AM	Moved off from WAVANS marched to SAULCHOY. Took over ten houses of 6 Cattle shed. we rebuilt on wood also took over 1 house from 6 M.G. Sqdn + 1 from 3 BSe. left three in ... Charge of 1 man at PONCHEL was to get a train at AUXI-LE-CHATEAU	
	25/9/16		Took over the 4 houses left at PONCHEL + ... 5 from AUXI-LE-CHATEAU. leaving left Hulland in Charge until arrival of train. (these 5 houses were at STABÉVILLE by R.T.O. sent ... our Patron she for FORGES-LES-FAUX.) Took over 2 houses from 5th Royal at RAYE	
	26/9/16		Took over 6 houses from N.S.Y. for reservation. Received 8 from HELOIN GEORGES-LES-FAUX sent Cpl Wilson there soon by mail to HANGEST to move the two houses in LEMEIGE + One in SOUES upstairs and at HANGEST to FORGES-LES-FAUX. A.D.V.S. multi ...	

WAR DIARY
or
INTELLIGENCE SUMMARY.
(Erase heading not required.)

Army Form C. 2118.

Place	Date	Hour	Summary of Events and Information	Remarks and references to Appendices
SAULCHOY	26/9/16		Took over 1 horse from 3 Siy. SydnRS. & from 4th Bde RHA ammn lot. JRS	
"	27/9/16		Took over 1 horse from HQrs 4th Bde RHA. Lieut Wilson arrived from HANGEST saying his head qrs were away from POUFI or LAMEGGE. JRS	
"	28/9/16		Visited all units under my charge & took over horse transportation. Evacuated to hospital from HEIDON Revd 1 from N.S.Y morning + 1 from 3 Lt. Syphn RF (aft) in afternoon. Reorder instruction to move in morning. JRS	
"	29/9/16	12 Noon	Moved off from SAULCHOY & arrived at CUCQ at 5pm. nection billeted in two farms. JRS	
CUCQ	30/9/16		Routine training up billets. JRS	

WAR DIARY
or
INTELLIGENCE SUMMARY.
(Erase heading not required.)

Army Form C. 2118.

Place.	Date	Hour	Summary of Events and Information	Remarks and references to Appendices
CUCQ	1 10/16		Visited units under my charge. Rifle Inspection. JRS.	
	2 10/16		Watson came down was on charge from 1st Royals. N° S.E. 3462 Pte TURNER. G.T. returned to duty from N° 2 V.A.Hr. JRS. Inspected Kit. JRS.	
	3 10/16			
	4 10/16		Took one kit horse to N.S.V. station. 6th 9 Septr. JRS.	
	5 10/16		Read two men from 1st Royals. Inspected Gasholmets. JRS.	
	6 10/16		Evacuated Stevenwich to N° 13 Vety Hpd NEUFCHATEL by road. Took over	
	7 10/16		64 Men N.S.V. Inoculations. JRS.	
	8 10/16		Routine Church Parade. JRS.	
	9 10/16		Took on 3 horses from 1st Royals + 3 from N.S.V. JRS.	
	10 10/16		Took on 2 horses from 1st Royals. AD.V.S. visited section inspected horses + inoculations. JRS.	
	11 10/16		Evacuated 19 sick thro exit horse to NEUFCHATEL by road. Read one from C/Batty R.H.A. JRS.	
	12 10/16		Inspected cart wheels. Routine JRS.	

WAR DIARY
or
INTELLIGENCE SUMMARY.
(Erase heading not required.)

Army Form C. 2118.

Place	Date	Hour	Summary of Events and Information	Remarks and references to Appendices
CUCQ	13/10/16		S.E. 3613 Pte LAWRENCE visited Hpt. for dental treatment. JRJ	
	14/10/16		S.E. 4702 Pte JAMES. T.T. proceeded on 6 days leave to England. Saddle Repr reporting	
	15/10/16		Routine	
	16/10/16		Took over 1 sick horse from 3"Bde + our from 6"M. G. Sqdn. JRJ	
	17/10/16		Took over 3 horses from Royals. one from N.S.Y. A.D.V.S. visited Section inspected horses. JRJ	
	18/10/16		Evacuated 16 sick to rail base. GNEUFCHATEL NO S R 11 Cpl. WILTON C.J. and 6 NEU	
	19/10/16		NoS Hpt NEUFCHATEL for a curve in Clifty with Stewart Clifty Machine. JRJ	
	20/10/16		Took over one horse from Hq 8rs 6"Ca Bde. Cpl Wilton returned from NEUFCHATEL. JRJ	
	21/10/16		Took over one horse from 6"M. G. Sqdn. JRJ	
			Changed billets in CUCQ to other 400 yds N of Q in CUCQ. Collected one horse from "C" Batty R.H.A. JRJ	
	22/10/16		NoSE 4702 Pte James T.T. returned from leave. Took over one horse from N.S.Y. hospital Smoke Helmets JRJ	
	23/10/16		Took over 3 horse from Royals and 2 from M.M.P 3"Bde. One Le St Stephen van proceeded to No 2 O.M.V.S. & brought back float. Pow'd No 500 tumbrels & C D JRJ	
	24/10/16		Collected one horse from C Batty R.H.A. (float case) H.D.V.S. inspected sick horses JRJ	

WAR DIARY or INTELLIGENCE SUMMARY.
(Erase heading not required.)

Army Form C. 2118.

Instructions regarding War Diaries and Intelligence Summaries are contained in F.S. Regs., Part II. and the Staff Manual respectively. Title pages will be prepared in manuscript.

Place	Date	Hour	Summary of Events and Information	Remarks and references to Appendices
CUCQ	25/10/16		D.D.V.S Car Corps + A.D.V.S visited Section made inspection. Evacuees 8 horses to NEUFCHATEL by rail. Inspected stables. Made estimate of requirements for improving stables. Visits for Pole. JRJ	
	26/10/16		Evacuated one horse to NEUFCHATEL by float. N°SE 11659 Pte JONES H. transferred to N° 14 M.V.S. in exchange for N° 268 Pte RIBBENS G. from that Section. Sent in weekly return. Inspected Saddlery. JRJ	
	27/10/16		Returned Float to N° 2 D.M.V.S at HESMOND. Drew chest for hilbite rotables JRJ	
	28/10/16		Returned horses N.S.Y. and one. Drew chest for stables JRJ	
	29/10/16		N°SE 2968 Pte MUNSON F. proceeded 6 days leave to England JRJ	
	30/10/16		Routine JRJ.	
	31/10/16		Took over 3 horses from Royals. Two for Evacuation. One for treatment. One from N.S.Y. for evacuation. Rec'd two from N° 14 M.V.S. for evacuation A.D.V.S inspected sick for evacuation JRJ.	

WAR DIARY
or
INTELLIGENCE SUMMARY

Army Form C. 2118.

13t Mobile Veterinary Section. A.V.C.
November 1916

Vol 22

Place	Date	Hour	Summary of Events and Information	Remarks and references to Appendices
CUCQ	1.XI.16		Evacuated seven sick horses to NEUFCHATEL by road. JRB	
	2.XI.16		Kit inspection. Sent in return. JRB	
	3.XI.16		Routine. JRB.	
	4.XI.16		Drew oats with G.S. wagon for own stables. JRB.	
	5.XI.16		Routine. JRB.	
	6.XI.16		Drew for 6t/d with Rations. Sergt Stephens & Pte Duncan young at ETAPLES for dental treatment. JRB	
	7.XI.16		A.D.V.S. visited section. Inspected sick. Lost one horse from N.S.Y. for evacuation. JRB	
	8.XI.16		Saddle inspection. JRB	
	9.XI.16		Took over one horse from 3 DelightR8 & tested with mallein. JRB.	
	10.XI.16		Took over one horse from N.S.Y. Helpm for treatment. C Battery Horse died Post Mortem examination revealed presence of three calculi. JRB	
	11.XI.16		Routine improve stabling. JRB	
	12.XI.16		Rifle inspection. JRB	
	13.XI.16		SE 2968 Pte MUNSON. F returned from leave. No 268 Pte RIBBENS.G. detached	

WAR DIARY
or
INTELLIGENCE SUMMARY
(Erase heading not required.)

Army Form C. 2118.

13th Mobile Veterinary Section AVC
November 1916

Place	Date	Hour	Summary of Events and Information	Remarks and references to Appendices
CUCQ	13.XI.16		For duty with Div. School 3rd Can Div at MERLIMONT PLAGE by order of A.D.V.S. JRS	
	14.XI.16		Took over one horse from B Sqdn N.S.Y. JRS	
	15.XI.16		Rec'd four horses from No 20 Mob Vety Section for evacuation. A.D.V.S. visited section & inspected horses. No 25159 Pte. Young. R.G. attached hospital for dental treatment JRS	
	16.XI.16		Evacuated six horses to No. 13 V.H. NEUFCHATEL by road (including 4 rec'd from No 20 M.V.S. yesterday) JRS	
	17.XI.16		Saddlery inspection. JRS	
	18.XI.16		No SF 92.5.4 Pte SKELTON.A. evacuated to No. 6 Can Fd Amb with injured knee JRS	
	19.XI.16		Routine JRS	
	20.XI.16		Took over three horses from 6th M.G. Sqdn & one from 3rd D.C. JRS	
	21.XI.16		Took over one horse from Rayples one chgr. of Lt Col Pagell G.S.O. 3rd Cd. JRS	
	22.XI.16		Rec'd one chgr from B Sqdn N.S.Y. Sgt Wilson & 2 men proceeded to BRIMEUX to meet three horses from No 14 M.V.S. & brought them to this section. A.D.V.S. visited section & inspected horses for evacuation. JRS	
	23.XI.16		Evacuated 9 sick horses to NEUFCHATEL by road 3 of which were received from No 14 Mob Vety Section. D.D.V.S. visited Section in company with A.D.V.S. Returned one chargr	

Place	Date	Hour	Summary of Events and Information	Remarks and references to Appendices
CUCQ	23/11/16		4 Royals and 4 other ranks destroyed home of 3 Fd Sqdn R.E. which were sent in by ADVS on 9.XI.16 SE 8990 Cpl HUBBARD granted 10 days leave in England from 24/11/16 — 4/12/16 JRB	
	24/11/16		First inspection routine JRB	
	25/11/16		Routine JRB	
	26/11/16		Routine JRB	
	27/11/16		4 HOD ex Fd hospital	
	28/11/16		Fourteen two horse lectures one horse from 3rd Bde toneology belonging to Capt Thompson Sern O&Co JRB Fourteen two horse tour Royals, ten N.S.Y. + one from H/69 6th Cav Bde Lfl WILTON, + two men proceeded to BRINEUX to collect 3 horses from 114 M.V.S. but returned with only 2 as the N.C.O. from 114 M.V.S had left one horse en route as it was unable to travel 268 Pte RIBBENS returned from Fd School 3 Cav Div having relieved by a S.S.Sgt from 3rd Bde A.D.V.S inoculated action inspected horse presentation	
	29/11/16		Evacuated 8 sick to NEUFCHATEL two of them were from No 14 M.V.S. SE9254 PG KELTON reported fit for duty from No 6 Cav Fd Amb JRB	
	30/11/16		Two horses from 3 Fd Sqdn RE sent in for inoculation JRB	

Army Form C. 2118.

No 13 Mobile Veterinary Section for December 1916

Vol 2

WAR DIARY or INTELLIGENCE SUMMARY.
(Erase heading not required.)

Place	Date	Hour	Summary of Events and Information	Remarks and references to Appendices
CUCQ	1/12/16		Inspected Rifles & horseshoeing. JPR. Took over one horse (Strange Case) from N.S.Y. JPR.	
	2/12/16		Routine. JPR.	
	3/12/16		Drew 4, 300 ricked Rations. Rec'd 6 horses from "C" Batty R.H.A. JPR.	
	4/12/16		Cpl Walton + 2 men proceeded to BRIMEUX about over 5 horses from No 14 M.V.S. for evacuation. A.D.V.S. visited Section & inspected sick. JPR.	
	5/12/16		Evacuated 13 horses to NEUFCHATEL (including 4 from 14 M.V.S). Made P.M. on horse which died last night on arrival from 14 M.V.S. Took over one horse from N.S.Y. JPR.	
	6/12/16		No SE 8970 Sgt Hubbard 6 returned from leave. JPR.	
	7/12/16		Routine. JPR.	
	8/12/16		Kit inspection. JPR.	
	9/12/16		Routine.	
	10/12/16			
	11/12/16		Took over for evacuation 3 from 6 M.G. Sqdn. 6 from Royals + 2 from Div. H.T. Coy 3CD attached to "C" Sqdn N.S.Y. Returned half Thompson's charger a curb & one to 6th M.G. Sqdn. in exchange. Drew 4, 300 in Pt Cabin. JPR.	
	12/12/16		Capt Davis acty A.D.V.S. visited Section. JPR.	

WAR DIARY
or
INTELLIGENCE SUMMARY.
(Erase heading not required.)

Army Form C. 2118.

No 13 Mobile Veterinary Section
for December 1916

Place	Date	Hour	Summary of Events and Information	Remarks and references to Appendices
CUCQ	13/12/16		Evacuated 11 sick to NEUFCHATEL. Cpl WILTON + 3 men proceeded to BRIMEUX to meet 4 horses from No 14. M.V.S. for evacuation. Billeted one horse (foot) from b/M. B. Egan. Returned one horse to Royals as fit for duty with cataract. Pte DURRAN. oldest soldier of party who was with Sergt Stephens 4.9 to NEUFCHATEL the morning on return at 2.45 P.M. reported Sergt STEPHENS had been arrested charged with Drunkenness + detained at GUARD ROOM of REST CAMP ETAPLES. JRS	
	14/12/16		Took one three horse from "C" Batty R.H.A. Sent escort to ETAPLES for Sergt Stephen on return reported Charge Sheet + Pay Book being sent on by post. Kept accused under close arrest. JRS	
	15/12/16		Evacuated 11 to NEUFCHATEL including crown of 14 M.V.S. Took over one from N.C.4 for treatment. JRS	
	16/12/16		Routine. JRS	
	17/12/16 18/12/16		Took over one cart horse from Sanitary Section. JRS Sergt Stephens placed under open arrest 48 hours having elapsed + charge sheet with to hand. Visited A.P.M. at ETAPLES + found charge sheet had been sent to No 13 Vety Hos. JRS. Drew 30 rations from Fd. Bakeries. JRS	
	18/12/16			

WAR DIARY or INTELLIGENCE SUMMARY

Army Form C. 2118.

No 13 Mobile Vety. Section for December 1916

Place	Date	Hour	Summary of Events and Information	Remarks and references to Appendices
CUCQ	19/12/16		Took over 14 horses from 38th (4 ektm 6 cost) 2 from NSY 2 from M.G. Sqdn. & 10 from Royals all cast. JRB	
	20/12/16		Evacuated 20 cast + 10 sick to NEUFCHATEL by road Sergt LUKEHURST.T.G. sent to No 6 Cav. Fd Amb. for treatment. JRB	
	21/12/16		T/33841 Dr CHAMBERLAIN A.E., A.S.C. Evacuated to ETAPLES with piles. One horse from 3.D.G's sent in as cast did it on own description on cart roll guard returned by me, & afterwards sent back by that Regt with an explanatory note. Statement of evidence signed by self together with Sergt STEPHENS pay book. Reported case to B.H. H.Q. was ordered to remand for a Court Martial. send him to M.M.P. 6 C.B. JRB	
CUCQ HESMOND	22/12/16	8 A.M. 2 PM	Left billets at C.U.C.Q & marched to HESMOND. Arrived in billets previously occupied by No 2 O.M.V.S. notified A.D.V.S. (hq onion of change of billets. JRB	
	23/12/16		No 726 Sergt LUKE HURST.T.G. returned to duty from No 6 Cav. Fd Amb. Fixed up new billets. No 608 Sergt STEPHEN S. F.G. handed over to M.M.P. 6 Res Bde ready Court Martial. JRB	
	24/12/16		No S.E. 5436 Pt BURRELL. W. sent to No 6 Cav. Fd Amb. with diarrhoea. JRB	
	25/12/16		Collected 4 horses from 3 Dny Gds at MARENLA completed stm over. JRB	

WAR DIARY
or
INTELLIGENCE SUMMARY.
(Erase heading not required.)

Army Form C. 2118.

No 13 Mobile Veterinary Section
for December 1916

Instructions regarding War Diaries and Intelligence Summaries are contained in F.S. Regs., Part II. and the Staff Manual respectively. Title pages will be prepared in manuscript.

Place	Date	Hour	Summary of Events and Information	Remarks and references to Appendices
HESMOND	26/12/16		A.D.V.S. visited suspected sick horse for evacuation. JRB	
	27/12/16		Collected one horse from SANOY N.S.Y. evacuated 10 to No 13 Vety Hosp NEUFCHATEL by rail. Staff Capt visited hills 40 & 79 to JAMES.T.T. visited ETAPLES for dental treatment No S.E. 9254 Pte SKELTON.H. proceeded on 10 days leave to England. Pte JAMES.T.T. and to ETAPLES to return to dental plate.	JRB
	28/12/16		Routine. Gas Helmet Inspection JRB	
	29/12/16		Attended Ride Halqu with four men to give evidence in case of Sergt Stephens	JRB
	30/12/16		Sergt Stephens taken over from H.M.P. brought to this Section. JRB	
	31/12/16		Cpl Welsh.G.J. & Pte Burrell proceeded to CVCQ to attend court of enquiry in the case of accident to SENIER EUGENE of MERLIMONT on 29.11.16. JRB	

J R Nelson Capt AVC
O.C. No 13 Mobile Vety Section

WAR DIARY
or
INTELLIGENCE SUMMARY.
(Erase heading not required.)

Army Form C. 2118.

Vol 24

No 13 Mob Vet Section

Place	Date	Hour	Summary of Events and Information	Remarks and references to Appendices
HESMOND	1/7/17		Took over four horses from 6th M.G. Sqdn, two from 4th Bde R.H.A., and two from Royals. Returned two unsound to N.S.Y. JPS	
	2/7/17		Took over one horse from N.S.Y. JPS	
	3/7/17		Evacuated 10 sick to NEUFCHATEL. Took over one from 3 D.G. one from G Batty R.H.A. JPS	
	4/7/17		Took over one horse from 6 M.G. Sqdn JPS	
PETIT BEAURAIN	5/7/17		Moved into billets at PETIT BEAURAIN, left HESMOND at 10 AM, arrived at 11 AM. Returned one horse to 2nd Lu Aux. H.T. Coy JPS	
	8/7/17		Took over four horses from Royals and one due H.T. Coy JPS	
	9/7/17		Took over four horses from N.S.Y., one from 6 M.G. Sqd H.Q.V.C. and spoilt sick JPS	
	10/7/17		Evacuated 10 sick to NEUFCHATEL JPS	
	12/7/17		SE19038 Sergt JOYES F.A. reported for duty from No 4 Vety Hosp Dublin JPS	
	15/7/17		Took over 2 horses from Royals JPS	
	16/7/17		Took over 1 from 'B' Batty R.H.A. JPS	
	17/7/17		Evacuated 4 to NEUFCHATEL JPS	
	22/7/17		Took over 1 horse from Royals & 1 from G Batty R.H.A. JPS	
	23/7/17		Took over 3 from 3 D.G. JPS	
	25/7/17		Evacuated 5 to NEUFCHATEL JPS	

Army Form C. 2118.

WAR DIARY
or
INTELLIGENCE SUMMARY.
(Erase heading not required.)

No 13 Mobile Vety Section

Place	Date	Hour	Summary of Events and Information	Remarks and references to Appendices
PETIT BEAURAIN	29/1/17		Returned one horse to 3 DG. JRS	
	30/1/17		Took over one horse from No 64 casualties from 3 DG. JRS	

J R William Lygrave
OC No 13 Mobile Vety Section

Vol 25

CONFIDENTIAL
WAR DIARY
of
No. 13 MOBILE VETERINARY SECTION

From 1 – 2 – 17   To 28 – 2 – 17

Army Form C. 2118.

WAR DIARY
or
INTELLIGENCE SUMMARY.
(Erase heading not required.)   No. 13 Mobile Vety. Section

Instructions regarding War Diaries and Intelligence
Summaries are contained in F. S. Regs., Part II.
and the Staff Manual respectively. Title pages
will be prepared in manuscript.

Place	Date	Hour	Summary of Events and Information	Remarks and references to Appendices
PETIT, BEAUVRAIN	2/1/17		4 Horses 3 home from N.S.Y. JRP	
	3/1/17		4 Horses 3 home from N.S.Y. JRP	
	8/1/17		Sent two home G.B.M.Q. Sqdn JRP	
	9/2/17		No T/2 10524 Dr ASHTON, A.T., A.S.C. reported for duty with 3 L.D. from H.Q. 6" Tr.Bn JRP	
	10/2/17		Recvd 1 G.S. draft from Royals JRP	
	12/2/17		4 Horses 1 home for Base Dépôt for treatment JRP	
	15/2/17		4 Horses 2 home from N.S.Y. to treatment now from 3 Bde JRP	
	25/2/17		4 Horses Workers from 3 D.G. to treatment. JRP	
	29/2/17		Took on horse from 3 Bde on strength JRP	

1 - 3 - 17.

J R Lillian Capt AVC
O.C. No. 13 Mobile Vety. Section

WAR DIARY
or
INTELLIGENCE SUMMARY
(Erase heading not required.)

Army Form C. 2118

No 13 Mobile Vety Section

Vol 2

Place	Date	Hour	Summary of Events and Information	Remarks and references to Appendices
PETIT BEAVRAIN	3/11		4 L.D. horses (influ) sent to 6th H. & Sqdn. JRB	
	6/11		9 sick returned cured to N.C.Y. + 1 (influ) handed to same Regt. JRB	
	13/11		1 horse returned to C from 2 DG	
	8/11		Moved to LA PAIX FAITE arriving in the following horses	
	20/11		(c Battery R.H.A. 3, 3rd Bry Sdn 11, N.C.Y 5, 2nd Div Am H.T. Bay 5, C Res Park 9. JRB	
LA PAIX FAITE	21/11		Evacuated 24 sick horses to No 13 V.H. Neufchatel by rail. JRB	
	22/11		Destroyed 3 horses of New H.T. Sec 15th Res Park C.W. JRB	
	23/11		Received the following ear horses. 3 Bde H. 6th G. Sqdn 3, N.S.Y. 9 Royals 9 including Major IRWIN's charger JRB	
	24/11 25/11		Evacuated 26 cast + 2 sick to No 13 V.H. Horses 1 chg from ok Cav Res Hosp goes Evacuated 1 chg to No 2 Baer Rent Depot Horses 3 from Royals came from 6 H.9 Sqdn JRB	
	26			
	27		4 horses 1 chg from G.H.Q. 2nd 1 chg to 14 D.Y.S. JRB	
	28		Horses 2 horses from N.S.Y. Evacuated 4 horses to NEUFCHATEL	

J.E. Allison Capt RAVC
O.C. No 13 Mob Vet Section

CONFIDENTIAL

War Diary
of

No. 13. Mobile Vety. Section.

From April 1st 1917   To April 30th 1917

Army Form C. 2118.

WAR DIARY
or
INTELLIGENCE SUMMARY.
(Erase heading not required.)

Rly ABBEVILLE
LENS

No. 13 Mob. Vety Section

Place	Date	Hour	Summary of Events and Information	Remarks and references to Appendices
LA PAIX FAITE	3/7/17		Took over horses from 3 DGs & one Mule from Chief Our HT boy. JR.	
	4/7/17		No. SE 8170 1/4 Cpl HUBBARD.G. AVC. despatched to HAVRE to report to OC Reinforcements Camp for R.G.A. JR. Four sick horses evacuated by road to No. 13 Vety Off NEUFCHATEL JR.	
BOUIN	5/7/17		Evacuated seven horses one mule by rail from MONTREUIL & joined Estb. at BOUIN. JR.	
	6/7/17		Took over 3 horses from N.S.Y, one from 6 M.G. Coy & 2 from 7 Royals JR.	
VACQUERIE-LE-BOUCQ	7/7/17		Evacuated six horses to No. 13 V.H. by rail from HESDIN marched with Bn to VACQUERIE-LE-BOUCQ. JR.	
	8/7/17		Took over ten horses from 3 DG marched under orders of ADVS joined Sid Troop at junction of BOUBERS-SUR-CANCHE – Pt BOUBERS – FREVENT and VACQUERIE-LE-BOUCQ – Pt BOUBERS – LIGNY-SUR-CANCHE roads and proceeded to GOUY-EN-ARTOIS when billets in hut Left one horse at 3 DG which was unable to travel at LIGNY-SUR-CANCHE. JR.	
GOUY-EN-ARTOIS	9/7/17		Left GOUY, & bivouaced on road between DUISANS and ARRAS at the E. in HALTE JR.	
ARRAS	10/7/17		Evacuated 5 horses to No. 20 MVS Proceeded with Bn Echelon at Sir & bivouaced near railway station at ARRAS No. SE 1436 Pte BAULCH HAVE joined Section. JR.	
ARRAS	11		Transport up and collected wounded stray horses in neighbourhood of ORANGE HILL also seven badly wounded. Six were driving wounded horses at RAILWAY STATION	

WAR DIARY
or
INTELLIGENCE SUMMARY.
(Erase heading not required.) No. 13 Mot. Vet. Section

Army Form C. 2118.

R₁/ ABBEVILLE 14 / 100000
LENS 11 / 100000

Place	Date	Hour	Summary of Events and Information	Remarks and references to Appendices
ARRAS	11/5/17		Horse fit for duty returned to Regt remainder evacuated to No 14 MVS. JPS	
	12/5/17		44 horses sent back to 14 MVS JPS	
	13		Section moved back to original bivouac at E. in HAUTIE in ARRAS-ST.POL road JPS	
	11-14		Party of men remained to look after in mislocation of ORANGE HILL + another corner of ARRAS - CAMBRI Road. JPS	
	15		Evacuated horses TABREVILLE in conjunction with 14 M.V.S. trypanoi Base at FOSSEUX Ricort + Puits JPS	
FOSSEUX	16		Proceeded to LEBOIGLE with Base. returned of R.H.Q. left at LEPONCHEL. The horses returned to 3 Bdes on fit for duty JPS	
	17		Returned 1 horse to Royals + attached NSV for duty. Recon on form Pas the Duc	
MAINTENAY	19		Evacuated 16 horses from HESDIN to NEUFCHATEL + then moved to MAINTENAY	
	20		3 horses returned to R.H.G. 1 to Lanc.Yrs 1 to Royals JPS	
	21		3 horses returned to R.M.Q Sqn. 1 belong to G.H. Battery R.H.A received from 6 M.G. Sqn JPS	
	22		Return 1 horse G.H. Batt.R.H.A. JPS	
	23		Took over 5 horses from C.Batt R.H.A 3 from Royals 2 from NSV JPS	
	24		3 " " 3 Bde 5 from NSV 1 from G.Batt Batt. and 1 from Huss. Sq 4 from R.H.A. JPS	
	25		1 " " N.S.Y. JPS	

Army Form C. 2118.

WAR DIARY
or
INTELLIGENCE SUMMARY. No 13 Mob Vety Section

(Erase heading not required.)

Instructions regarding War Diaries and Intelligence Summaries are contained in F. S. Regs., Part II. and the Staff Manual respectively. Title pages will be prepared in manuscript.

Place	Date	Hour	Summary of Events and Information	Remarks and references to Appendices
MAINTENAY	April 26		Promoted nom acct UNEUFCHATEL. Returned to duty 4 GC Bailey 16338 & 6th made HENEU	
			No SE 18863 Pte ROWLES. H. reported for duty from No 6 Vety Hpl & 906 Pte LUKEHURST and Pte N 2 Vety Hpl	
	27		No SE 11901 Pte HAYES W reported for duty from No 9 Vety Hpl. Yorktown / leave from N.Y GBD	
	28		No SE 9163 Pte WILLINGHAM, F. J. cald to No 2 Vety Hpl for duty	
	30		No 706 Sergt. MAVIN. W. reported from No 2.	

J.C. William Baffran
O.C. No 13 Mob Vety Section.

Army Form C. 2118.

WAR DIARY
or
INTELLIGENCE SUMMARY. No. 3 Mob. Vety. Section.
ABBEVILLE
(Erase heading not required.)
Ref LENS, AMIENS, ST QUENTIN

Vol II E 18

Instructions regarding War Diaries and Intelligence Summaries are contained in F. S. Regs., Part II. and the Staff Manual respectively. Title pages will be prepared in manuscript.

Place	Date	Hour	Summary of Events and Information	Remarks and references to Appendices
MAINTENAY	1.5.17		Took over 1 horse Royals + 8 from N.S.Y. JOB	
	2.5.17		Evacuated to NEUFCHATEL Estimated 3 GN.S.Y. JOB	
	8"		Took over 4 from N.S.Y., 5 from 3 B4s, 4 from Royals + 2 from C Rallye HA JOB	
	9"		Two Bricks reported for duty from A.T.C. Base Depot. JOB	
	10"		Evacuated 2 horses to NEUFCHATEL, that one 2 from 64 Q. Sep. reserved from N.S.Y. JOB	
	11"		by D.M.V.S JOB	
TORTEFONTAINE	12		Left MAINTENAY marched to TORTEFONTAINE JOB	
FROHEN-LE-GRAND	13		TORTEFONTAINE " FROHEN-LE-GRAND JOB	
HAVERNAS	14		Self & one Horse from N.S.Y. evacuated to FORGES-LES-EAUX from FREVENT. Marched to HAVERNAS JOB	
	15"		Horse from HAVERNAS to BUSSY-LES-DAOURS JOB	
BUSSY-LES-DAOURS	16		Took over 3 Bolt + 1 Sick from Royals & 1 sick from 2 DG, 1 Cash. from 64 QA & took 1 horse evacuated to NEUFCHATEL JOBURBE	
			Got new 1 horse for treatment from 4 DAC. JOB	
BAYONVILLERS	17		March from BUSSY-LES-DAOURS to BAYONVILLERS JOB	
	19		BAYONVILLERS to BUIRE JOB	
BUIRE	24		Took over 2 horses from N.S.Y for Treatment JOB	
	25"		Left over 4 cast horses for 3 Bfs JOB	
			" " " " from N.S.Y.	
			" " Blues	
			1 sick " " "	

2353   Wt. W3541/1454   700,000 5/15   D. D. & L.   A.D.S.S. Forms/C. 2118.

WAR DIARY
or
INTELLIGENCE SUMMARY.
(Erase heading not required.)

Army Form C. 2118.

No 13 Mob V du Section
Ref. ST QUENTIN 1/2 1/150000

Place	Date	Hour	Summary of Events and Information	Remarks and references to Appendices
BUIRE	26/5/17		Innoculated 115 O.R. Two sect. for TINCOURT & FORGES-LES-EAUX JRB	
	28/5/17		No 2917 Pte BARRIE J. reported for duty from No 1 VAC MAC JRB	
	30/5/17		Hot Water shower from N&Y JRWilson	

J.R.William Laprave
O.C. No 13 Mob. Vety Section

WD

N129

Confidential
War Diary
of
No. 13 Mobile Vety Section

From June 1st 1917
To June 30th 1917

WAR DIARY or INTELLIGENCE SUMMARY.

Army Form C. 2118.

No 13 Mob Vety Section.
R. ST QUENTIN

(Erase heading not required.)

Place	Date	Hour	Summary of Events and Information	Remarks and references to Appendices
BUIRÉ	1/VI/19		Took over 1 Chg from A.S.C 3rd Co bn 1 hm 3rd Sig Sqn R.E. 1 horse fm N.S.Y. 1 from Royals Coln from 3 Det. JAY	
	2/VI		Evacuated 10 horses to FORGES-LES-EAUX JAY	
	5		Taken on lodn from N.S.Y. JAY	
	6		Taken on loan from A.H.P 3 Co. B.C. on Emerg. in Charge of Hosp. 6 T.C. Pde. JAY	
	8		Tk over 1 horse fm N.S.Y. + 1 fm Royals JAY	
	9		Evacuated 11 to FORGES-LES-EAUX	
	10			
	11		Took over 1 from Battalion JAY	
	12		1 . 3DGs JAY	
	13		1 . NSY	
	18		1 . . NSY	
	19		Evacuated 6 to FORGES-LES-EAUX JAY	
	22		Returned one horse to Royals JAY	
	27		Took over 1 horse fm 6 Signal Troop JAY	
	29/VI		4 Royals 3 fm 5 DGs 1 fm MGC Sqn + 1 fm N.S.Y. Board 1 remount JAY	
	30/VI		Evacuated 14 horses to FORGES-LES-EAUX JAY	

WL 30

Confidential
War Diary
of

No. 13 Mobile Vety Section

From 1st July 1917   to 31st July 1917

No. 13 Mobile Veterinary Section

Army Form C. 2118.

Reg 36A 1/49000

WAR DIARY
or
INTELLIGENCE SUMMARY.
(Erase heading not required.)

Place	Date	Hour	Summary of Events and Information	Remarks and references to Appendices
BUIRE	3/7/17	AM 7.30	Left BUIRE and arrived at SUZANNE. JPR	
SUZANNE	4/7/17	9.30	Left SUZANNE marched to HEILLY JPR	
HEILLY	5/7/17		Marched to ORVILLE, Took over 1 horse from H.G. Septr, one from 3 Fd Lgh troop from 3 DG + two N.S.Y. JPR	
ORVILLE	6/7/17		Took over one horse from 3 Bde transmitter of to ABBEVILLE from DOULLENS. marched to REBREUVIETTE JPR	
REBREUVIETTE	7/7/17		Marched to AUCHEL JPR	
AUCHEL	12/7/17		Took over the following horses Three 30th, 3 Royals, three 6HG + two N.S.Y. JPR	
	13/7/17		Took over one horse from Royals transmitted return to NEUFCHATEL from BRUAY, collected one mule	
	15/7/17		Left by 20 D.A.C. at NEDONCHELLE JPR Histories onboard of typical Tomb, one 6H.G.Sqd evacuated with gunshot wound to NEUFCHATEL from BRUAY	
	16/7/17		Marched to MERVILLE + billeted with gunshot wounds at LES LAURIES	
MERVILLE	18/7/17		Moved billet to LES PURESBECQUE'S JPR	
LES PURESBECQUE	21/7/17		Inspection by O.C. 6th Corps JPR	
	23/7/17		Took over 1 N.S.Y + 1 Am Bosch JPR	

Army Form C. 2118.

WAR DIARY
or
INTELLIGENCE SUMMARY.

No 13 Mob Vety Section

Ref Shut 36ᴬ 1/40000

(Erase heading not required.)

Instructions regarding War Diaries and Intelligence Summaries are contained in F. S. Regs., Part II. and the Staff Manual respectively. Title pages will be prepared in manuscript.

Place	Date	Hour	Summary of Events and Information	Remarks and references to Appendices
LFS	26/7/17		Took over 2 hor Ranch 1 from N 9 Sqn & from 3 Sqn, 8 cart from C Batty RHA 1 from N Y & 14 MP 6th Cav Bde XPI	
PURFESBECQUES	27/7/17		Evacuated 8 cases & 16 sick to Base XPI	

J R Allison Lagrave
O.C. Nº 13 Mob Vety Section

Vol 31

Confidential
War Diary
of
No. 13 Mobile Vety Section

From 1st August 1914
To 31st Augt 1914.

WAR DIARY or INTELLIGENCE SUMMARY

No. 13 Mob. Vety. Station
Army Form C. 2118.
Rd Sheet 36ᴬ 1/40,000

Place	Date	Hour	Summary of Events and Information	Remarks and references to Appendices
LES PUBESBECQUES	2/8/17		Evacuated 2 horses from Royals to one from N.S.Y. J.R.¹	
	3/8/17		Evacuated 2 to ABBEVILLE J.R.¹	
	10/8/17		Evacuated one case of epidemic mange & isolated two Royals. J.R.¹	
	14/8/17		Evacuated 1 horse from N.S.Y. J.R.¹	
	16/8/17		Took over one horse from 6 Field Trenp, 3 from Royals 6 from 3 Sec 3 Army. J.R.¹	
	17/8/17		Evacuated 12 to ABBEVILLE. J.R.¹	
	20/8/17		Evacuated one from N.S.Y for isolation. J.R.¹	
	21/8/17		Returned two to N.S.Y. J.R.¹	
	26/8/17		Destroyed one horse as incurable. J.R.¹	
	27/8/17		Took over in hand from 3 Sec¹ one from Royals & five from N.S.Y. J.R.¹	
	28/8/17		Evacuated 9 to ABBEVILLE, returned 1 to Royals & 1 to N.S.Y. Sold horseflesh for 20 210 /P.¹	
	30/8/17		Took over one horse from C. Batty R.H.A. for treatment. J.R.¹	

J.W. Johnstone
O.C. No 13 Mob Vety Station

WAR DIARY or INTELLIGENCE SUMMARY

No. 13 Mobile Vety Section   Army Form C. 2118.

Ref/Mob 36/A/1 M.G.V.O.   September 1917

Vol 3 2

Place	Date	Hour	Summary of Events and Information	Remarks and references to Appendices
LES PURESBECQUES	1/9/17		Took over workhorse from "C" Batty R.H.A. JRS	
	2/9/17		Left over one from Amm fol 3rd Cav Div and two H.M.P.G for Rec, one from Sigts and one from 6th H.Q. Sign received from 3rd Cav Div Reserve Park JRS/J.	
	3/9/17		Proceeded Phones to a mule to No 32 Vety. Hosp ABBEVILLE. Took one out from Amm Fd/Bde JRS.	
	4/9/17		Took one 3 from Royals, one from Sigts, one from Amm Col 3rd Cav Div, + one mule from 2nd Cav Div Reserve Park JRS.	
	9/9/17		Inoculated 6 horses received from No 22 V. H. ABBEVILLE	
	10/9/17		Took one following returned: 4 - 3rd Bde, 7 - Royals, 11 N.S.Y. 8 - Amm Col 2 Cav Div JRS	
	11/9/17			
	13/9/17		Inoculated 32 & Atturvilles returned one from 20 M.V.S. JRS	
	14/9/17		Collected 1 H.D. from 1st Army Aux Horse JRS	
	16/9/17		Took one 6 from N.S.Y. + 3 from Royals, 2 from Amm Col + 2 cart from 3rd Coy Square JRS	
	17/9/17		Took one from 6th H.Q. Sqn JRS.	
	18/9/17		Proceeded 16 to Atturvilles took one, from C Batty 121 Bde R.F.A. JRS	
	20/9/17		Took one out from 6 Signal Troop, one from C Batty 121 Bde R.F.A. JRS	
	21/9/17		Took one 1 from Royals JRS	
	24/9/17		Took one 3 Royals, 2 Amm Col, 1 N.S.Y. + 1 from Anglo ATC 3 Cav Div JRS	
	25-9-17		Proceeded 9 to Atturville JRS	

J.P. Williams Cosgrove
O/C No 13 Mob Vety Section

WAR DIARY or INTELLIGENCE SUMMARY

Army Form C. 2118.

No. 13 Mob. Vety. Sectn.
ABBEVILLE 14.
October 1917
Rf. Hoglmounts 6"A ABBEVILLE 14.
LENS. 1/10000.

WP 33

Place	Date	Hour	Summary of Events and Information	Remarks and references to Appendices
LES PURESBECQUES	1·10·17		Restored one horse from 3rd for Div. Ammn. Col., 3 from 1st Royals, 2 from 3 Bde JRA	
	2·10·17		Restored one team 1st Army AHT (on transmutation @ ABBEVILLE) took over 1 tm 6th M.G. Coy and from 3 Bde JRA	
	5·10·17		Returned one charger to Royals for duty took over one horse from N.S.Y. JRA	
	8·10·17		Restored 4 Royals, 4 N.S.Y., 6 O.R. Bde JRA	
	9·10·17		Evacuated 18 ABBEVILLE JRA	
	10·10·17		Evacuated pneumonia from Ampl. Tk. Coy JRA	
	11·10·17		Took over 13 horses from 6th Coy Bde Amb. E.A.Coy took over 2 from Royals JRA	
	12·10·17		Took over one charger from Hodge Gl. for Bde evacuated 16 ABBEVILLE JRA	
	15·10·17		Restored two from N.S.Y. & 38 from Ammn. Tk. Bttty JRA	
	16·10·17		Got one on from 3 Brig Gds.	
	17·10·17		Restored 15 horses of Amnt Reatly +3 from N.S.Y. & handed over to 14 M.V.S. for evacuation	
TANGRY	19·10·17		LEFT LES PURESBECQUES at 5:30 AM marched over bridge over Canal D'AIRE à LA PASSE on ST. VENANT — BUSNES reached at 8:15 AM marched to TANGRY	
HONVAL	22·10·17		Left TANGRY at 4:30 PM marched to HONVAL JRA	
	23·x·17		Mard from HONVAL & marched to GORENFLOS JRA	

Army Form C. 2118.

WAR DIARY
or
INTELLIGENCE SUMMARY.

No 13 Mob Vety Section

October 1917

(Erase heading not required.)

Instructions regarding War Diaries and Intelligence Summaries are contained in F. S. Regs., Part II. and the Staff Manual respectively. Title pages will be prepared in manuscript.

Place	Date	Hour	Summary of Events and Information	Remarks and references to Appendices
GORENFLOS	24.X.17	9.15	Left GORENFLOS marched to COCQUEREL (R)	
COCQUEREL	29.X.17		Took over one horse from N.S.V. and 6 from 14 M.V.S (R)	
	30.X.17		Took over 3 from 3 Bray Sqdn, one from APM 2nd Ly Div and 60 from 11th Posh Ammn Col. Evacuated ten to ABBEVILLE by road (R)	

A R Allison Capt AVC
OC No 13 Mob Vety Section

Confidential
War Diary
of
No. 13 Mobile H.Q. Section.

From Nov. 1st 1917.   to Nov. 25th 1917.

WAR DIARY or INTELLIGENCE SUMMARY

No. 13 Mobile Vety. Section
November 1917
Rly. ABBEVILLE 14

Army Form C. 2118.

Place	Date	Hour	Summary of Events and Information	Remarks and references to Appendices
COCQUEREL	3/XI/17		Puis out at then loose at ABBEVILLE took over from No 3 Mob: Vety. Sectn. C/o O.C. L.C. RYAN.	
	6/XI/17		A.V.C. reported for duty from A.V.D. No III. Lt. Col. D.S.G.	
			Took over on truck from 3rd Cav. Div. Reserve Sectn. & on loan from 3rd Cav. Div. Sup. Sqn.	
	7/XI/17		Capt. J. REALLISON proceeded to No 6 Vety. Hosp. ROUEN for duty. O/CR.	
	8/XI/17		Took over on loan from 3rd Army G.H. for treatment. O/CR.	
			Evacuation from No 22 Vety Hosp ABBEVILLE. Transferred on G.S. Bks. Std. Stn.	
			horses to M.S.Y. O/CR.	
	9/XI/17		Took over horse from 1st Reserve. O/CR.	
	11/XI/17		Took over horse from 3rd Cav. Div. Amm. Col. O/CR.	
	12/XI/17		Took over eight horses on truck from 1st Reserve. On tram 3rd Cav Div Res. H.T. Cy.	
			on tram 6th M.G. Sqn. him M.S.Y. & on 3rd Army G.H.	
	13/XI/17		Evacuation sightlier horses & two trucks to No 22 Vety. Hosp. ABBEVILLE. O/CR.	
	14/XI/17		Collected horse left by "C" Batty. R.H.A. at AILLY-LE-HAUT-CLOCHER. O/CR.	
	15/XI/17		Took over four horses from 1st Reserve. Three from M.S.Y. & two 6th M.G. Sqn. O/CR.	
	16/XI/17		Evacuation sixteen to No 22 Vety. Hosp. ABBEVILLE. O/CR.	
	17/XI/17		Left COCQUEREL at 8.30 A.m. & Marched to BEAUCOURT-SUR-HALLUE.	

Clement S.C. Ryan Captain

WAR DIARY or **INTELLIGENCE SUMMARY.**

Army Form C. 2118.

(Erase heading not required.)

No. 11. 4 AMIENS.17 1/100,000 13" M.V.S.

NOVEMBER 1917

Place	Date	Hour	Summary of Events and Information	Remarks and references to Appendices
	18.17		Left BEAUCOURT-SUR-HALLUE at 4 p.m. & marched to BUZANNE. C/CR	
	21.		Took over one horse HA Bo. 6th Cav. Bde. one from 3rd Stray Gds & five from 1st Royals. C/CR	
	22nd		Left BUZANNE & marched to TALMAS. C/CR	
	26.		Collected no horses. Travelling from 3rd Fd. Sqn. R.E. C/CR	
	27.		Took over two horses from 3rd Fd. Sqn. & one from 1st Royals. e/CR	
	28.		Collected horses from CONTAY which was left by 1st Royals on line of march. C/CR	
			Returned one to HA. Bo. 6th Cav. Bde. for duty & took over one from H.B.Y. C/CR	
	30.		Took over three from M.S.Y. One from 3rd Stray Gds. & two trustee from 3rd Cav Div Roraux Pack. e/CR	

Lieut J.C. Ryan
Capt RVC

Vol 35

CONFIDENTIAL
War Diary
of
No. 13 Mobile Vety Section

From 1=12=14.   To. 31=12=14.

Ref. L.E NB SHEET II AMIENS IV.
1/100,000   1/100,000

Army Form C. 2118.

13th Mobile Veterinary Section

WAR DIARY
or
INTELLIGENCE SUMMARY.
(Erase heading not required.)

Instructions regarding War Diaries and Intelligence Summaries are contained in F.S. Regs., Part II. and the Staff Manual respectively. Title pages will be prepared in manuscript.

Place	Date	Hour	Summary of Events and Information	Remarks and references to Appendices
THLMAS	1/12/17		Evacuated cardiac broken and two mules to ABBEVILLE. C/CR.	
	2/12/17		Lt-Col. Willats of THLMAS and we left for MOLLIENS-AU-BOIS. C/CR.	
MOLLIENS-AU-BOIS	7/12/17		Handed over one horse "Lonsdale" to 33 Divn Cav. H.Q. C/CR.	
	8/12/17		Took over two horses from 1st Royals and four from 3rd Troop G.H.Q. C/CR.	
	9/12/17		Took over two horses from North Irish Horse. C/CR.	
	10/12/17		Took over one horse from L.M.G. Sqn and three mules from 3rd Cav Div Pioneer Bn. C/CR.	
	12/12/17		Took over five horses from R.E.H. and six from 3rd Tpy Gen Beaumetz Divn. C/CR.	
			to ABBEVILLE. C/CR.	
	13/12/17		Evacuated one horse cursed of Lymphangitis to 6th M.V. Sqn at Mods. C/CR.	
			Took over one horse from L.H. C/CR.	
	14/12/17	BGH	Took two horses from 1st Car H. Bgde and one from R.E.H. C/CR.	
	15/12/17		Took over two from M.B.G.Y. C/CR.	
	16/12/17		Evacuated execration horses to ABBEVILLE. Return our 6 cases to 1st Royals. C/CR.	
	17/12/17		Took over one mule from 3rd Cav. Pioneer Bn which was found straying. C/CR.	
	21/12/17		Left MOLLIENS-AU-BOIS + marched to COCQUEREL. Took over one horse from 3rd Troop G.H.Q.	
COCQUEREL.	23/12/17		Took over two horses from 1st Royals. C/CR.	
			C/C Ryan Capt AVC	

Aug. 1918. II
AMIENS. 14.

WAR DIARY
or
INTELLIGENCE SUMMARY.
(Erase heading not required.)

Army Form C. 2118.

13th Mobile Veterinary Section

Place	Date	Hour	Summary of Events and Information	Remarks and references to Appendices
BOVQUEREL	24/15		Took over two horses from 1st Royals and one from 3rd Dgs Gds + one from 6th M.O. Sqd. M.R.	
	26"		Returned one horse to 3rd Dragoon Gds. for duty. e/c R.	
	27"		J.J.S. practice parties and horse e/c R.	
	28"		Evacuated seven sick horses to ABBEVILLE. e/c R.	
	29"		Handed over one truck horse belonging to 3rd Can. Div. Reserve Pk. e/c R.	
	30"		Took over one horse from 6th M.G. Sqd. e/c R.	
	31"		Took over one horse from 6th M.G. Sqd. e/c R.	

C.C. Ryan Capt. AVC.

Vol 36

CONFIDENTIAL

WAR DIARY OF

No 13 Mobile Vety Section

From 1-1-18   To 31-1-18.

WAR DIARY
or
INTELLIGENCE SUMMARY

(Erase heading not required.)

Army Form C. 2118.

Reference. 1/50,000. ABBEVILLE. 14.

Instructions regarding War Diaries and Intelligence Summaries are contained in F.S. Regs., Part II. and the Staff Manual respectively. Title pages will be prepared in manuscript.

Place	Date	Hour	Summary of Events and Information	Remarks and references to Appendices
COCQUEREL	1.4.18		Took over our horse from 6th M.G. Sqn. three from 1st Royals & three from 3rd Dragoon Gds. e/cR	
	3"		Took over three horses from 3rd Dragoon Gds. e/cR.	
	5"		A.D. & S. inspected sick horses e/cR	
	6"		Took over one charger from H.Q. Gds. 3rd Cav. Div. one horse from 6th Cav. Bde. Sig Troop & one mule from Hq. A.L. Coy. 3rd Cav. Div. e/cR.	
	7"		Took over one from M.B.14 Fd Amb & evacuated one to No.14 Shy Hospl ABBEVILLE, who had # No.14 M.M.S horse e/cR.	
	10"		Retired one to 6th M.G. Sqn. cured of Ophthalmia & returned one to 6th C.B. Hd. Qr	
	11"		Transferred one L.D. to Leicester Yeomanry. Took over one from 1st Royals. e/cR.	
	16"		Took over 2 brown cob horses from 2nd Royals & one from 3rd Dray Gds. & one M.S.Y.	
	17"		Took over three horses from 1st Royals & one from 6th Cav Bde. 3rd Dry Gds.	
	18"		& one 6th M.G. Sqn. A.D.& S. inspected sick horses e/cR	
	19"		Evacuated 22mm sick horses to No.14 Shy Hospl ABBEVILLE e/cR.	
			Took over two horses from 1st Royals & one from 6th M.G. Sqn. e/cR.	
			S.R.M Corpl. WILTON C.T.C. (A.V.C.) evacuated to No. 2 Stationary Hosp. ABBEVILLE	
	24"		Took over one horse from 6th M.G. Sqn. & one from M.M.P. 6th Cav. Bde A.D.&S. inspected sick horses e/cR.	

Clement J.E. Regan. Capt. A.V.C

WAR DIARY
or
INTELLIGENCE SUMMARY.
(Erase heading not required.)

Army Form C. 2118.

Ref: 10D, O.T.O.
ABBEVILLE. 14.
r. 1/40, c=b. 6 2. C.

Place	Date	Hour	Summary of Events and Information	Remarks and references to Appendices
COQUEREL	25/18		Took over his horse from 13th Regt: L.H. Regt. + one from 3rd Drag. Gds. 2/CR	
	26th		Took our his horse from M.S.V. six from 1st Royals + one from 6th Cav. Fd. Amb.	
			Returned one to 1st Royals + evacuated thirteen to No. 14 Stat Hosp. ABBEVILLE. CCR	
	27th		Evacuated one M.S.V. one 3rd Drag Gds. + one 1st Royals	
			by Ambulance to No. 14 Stat. Hosp. ABBEVILLE. CCR	
	28th		Left COQUEREL at 10 A.M. + marched to BELLOY-SUR-SOMME. Took over one	
			horse from 6th M.C. Sqd. + one from 1st Royals + one from M.M.P. 6th Cav. Bde. 2/CR	
BELLOY-SUR-SOMME	29th		Evacuated sick horse to M.14 Stat Hosp ABBEVILLE. Left BELLOY-SUR-SOMME	
			at 8 A.M. + marched to MARCEL-CAVE. c/cR	
	30		Left MARCEL-CAVE at 8. A.M. + marched to TERTRY. 2/CR.	
TERTRY.	31st		Took over one horse which was found straying in 1st Royals lines. 2/CR	

Clement J.P. Ryan Capt A.V.C.

Confidential.
War Diary.
No. 13. Mobile Vety. Section.

From 1:2:18.
To 28:2:18.

Reference Sheet 62.C. Army Form C. 2118.

WAR DIARY
or
INTELLIGENCE SUMMARY.
(Erase heading not required)

1:40,000

Instructions regarding War Diaries and Intelligence Summaries are contained in F. S. Regs., Part II. and the Staff Manual respectively. Title pages will be prepared in manuscript.

Place	Date	Hour	Summary of Events and Information	Remarks and references to Appendices
TERTRY	1/2/18		Took over Horses from 34th Brono Horse Rgt. R.H.H.Q. inspected sick animals	e/CR
	2nd		Took over 15 horses from "U" Batty R.H.A. Had mule from H.Q. 1st Cav. Bde. + returned on horse to 3rd Drag Gds. "Greys" G Tonge	e/CR
	3rd		Took over 10 horses from 3rd Drag Gds. + one travelling from M.M.P. 6th Cav. Bde.	e/CR
	4th		Took over one LD horse from 8th Cav. Fd. Amb. + his from 5th Fd. Sqdn. R.E.	e/CR
	5th / 6th		Returned on travelling at M.M.P. 6th Cav. Bde.	e/CR
			Took over one horse from "Q" Batty R.H.A. One from "K" Batty + his from "E" Batty R.H.H.	e/CR
	7th		Took over three horses from 12th Royal. One from 3rd Sig. Sqn. + seven mules from 3rd Cav. Div. Lorrow Park	e/CR
	8th		Evacuation twelve horses + seven mules to Mr. V. Vety. Hospl. FORGES-LES-EAUX.	e/CR
	11th		Took over three horses from "J" Batty R.H.A. One from 6th Cav. Fd. Amb.	e/CR
	12th		Took over one horse from Hd. Qrs. 8th Cav. Bde.	e/CR
	13th		Took over three horses from 14th Bde. R.H.A. + Amm. Colum. One from 6th M.G. Sqn. + three from "U" Batty R.H.A.	e/CR
			Lt. Ryan left here	

WAR DIARY
or
INTELLIGENCE SUMMARY.
(Erase heading not required.)

Reference Sheet 62.C. Army Form C. 2118.
1.40,000

Instructions regarding War Diaries and Intelligence Summaries are contained in F. S. Regs., Part II. and the Staff Manual respectively. Title pages will be prepared in manuscript.

Place	Date	Hour	Summary of Events and Information	Remarks and references to Appendices
TERTRY	14th	7	Took over lines drawn from M.S.Y. horse from 1st Bn. 3rd Dragoons.	ELCR
	15th	4	Sent over one horse from 5th Yd. Sqn. R.S.	ELCR
	16th		Took over this horse from 12th Royal. No.7/2942. Pr. WILLIAMS. R. evacuated to Hospital	ELCR
	17th		Took over one horse from M.S.Y.	ELCR
	18th		Sent over one horse from "E" Batty R.H.A. H.S.B.S. inspected sick animals	ELCR
	19th		Evacuated sick horse to M. & Vet. Hosp'l. FORGES-LES-EAUX	ELCR
	21st		Took over one horse from 8th M.B. Sqn.	ELCR
	24th		Handed over No's to D. Hawks "Jardlings" to 3rd Cav. Div. Remn. Park.	ELCR
	25th		Took over one stray horse from "E" Batty R.H.A. + two from 5th Fd. Sqn. R.S.	ELCR
	26th		Took over one horse from 6th M.C. Bn.	ELCR
	27th		Sent over one horse driven from "U" Batty R.H.A.	ELCR
	28th		Took over three horses from M.S.Y.	ELCR
				ℓ/c Ryan-Lft Ave.

CONFIDENTIAL

WAR DIARY

OF

No.13 MOBILE VETY SECTION.

From 1-3-18   To. 31-3-18

Reference 8 tel b 2 C.

Army Form C. 2118.

WAR DIARY
or
INTELLIGENCE SUMMARY.
(Erase heading not required)

Instructions regarding War Diaries and Intelligence Summaries are contained in F. S. Regs., Part II. and the Staff Manual respectively. Title pages will be prepared in manuscript.

Place	Date	Hour	Summary of Events and Information	Remarks and references to Appendices
TERTRY	1.3.18		Evacuated 9 horses to Mob. Vet. Hosp. FORGES-LES-EAUX. Relieved on lines by R Batty R.H.A. cavd of Farrgt. C/CR	
	4.		Took over two good horses from 3rd Stry Gds. Also from W/Batty R.H.A. w/from H.S.T. & C. & from 141st Labour Coy. & Mun from 1st Royals C/CR	
	5.		Evacuated slight horses to FORGES-LES-EAUX C/CR	
	6.		Took over our horse from Q Batty R.H.A C/CR	
	7.		Took over our horse R.C.H. Ammunition Column, on 3rd Stry Gds. on W/ B.Y and two from 1st Royals C/CR	
	8.		Capt. C/C RYAN, proceeded to Mob Vety Hospl ROUEN to course of instruction in Bacteriology	
	9.			
	10.			
	11.		Took over two horses from 3rd Stry Gds. & w from 1st Royals A.D.V.8 inspection sick horses C/CR	
	12.		Evacuated two horses to Mob. y Vety Hospl FORGES-LES-EAUX C/CR	
DEVISE	13.		Left TERTRY & marched to DEVISE C/CR	
	14.		Took over four horses from 16th Bde R.H.A Amn Column. C/CR	
	15.		Took over our horse from 23rd I.A Bde L/CR	
	16.		Took over two horses from 108th Batty 23rd I.A.Bde. & w from 6th M.G Sqd. and from 11th R. Hussars. Our two 16th Bde R.H.A & wx two from 23rd I.A.R Bde.	
	17.		Took over our horse from the 11th Cav Bde & w from 104th Batty 23rd Bde R.H.A. M.B.E.3613. Pt. LAWRENCE.A.V.C. Evacuated to Hospl C/CR Capt. C.f.C.RYAN. returned from Mob. Vet. Hospl ROUEN. C/CR Clement J. Ryan	

M.S.E. 3613. Pt. LAWRENCE.A.V.C.

(A7091). W.W12859/M1293. 75,000. 1/17. D.D. & L., Ltd. Forms/C218/14.

Army Form C. 2118.

References: Sheet 62.E. " AMIENS. Scale 1/100,000.
" Sheet 9.E. " 1/50,000.
" BEAUVAIS. 21.

WAR DIARY
or
INTELLIGENCE SUMMARY.
(Erase heading not required.)

Instructions regarding War Diaries and Intelligence Summaries are contained in F. S. Regs., Part II. and the Staff Manual respectively. Title pages will be prepared in manuscript.

Place	Date	Hour	Summary of Events and Information	Remarks and references to Appendices
DEVISE	18/8/18		Took over 1st Horse from 6th M.G. Sqn. Also two from 1st Royals & one "C" Batty R.H.A. Also H.Q. Batts. R.H.A. & Ah. Col. 6th Cav. Bde. & on 23rd of L.A. Bde.	
	19th		Took over on horse from 1st Royals & on 6th M.G. Sqn. Evacuation twenty seven horses to No. 4 Vy. Hosp. FORGES-LES-EAUX.	
	20th		Took over one horse from 17th Bde. R.H.A. Amm. Column.	
	21st		Took over one horse from 16th Bde R.H.A. Destroyed one 21st Royal Dragoons.	
BEAUMONT-EN-BIENE	22nd		2 L.H. DEVISE & marched to BEAUMONT-EN-BIENE.	
PONTOISE	23rd		O. L.H. BEAUMONT-EN-BIENE & marched to PONTOISE.	
CARLEPONT	25th		O. L.H. PONTOISE & marched to CARLEPONT.	
OLLENCOURT	26th		O. L.H. CARLEPONT & marched to OLLENCOURT.	
CHOISY	27th		O. L.H. OLLENCOURT & marched to CHOISY.	
			Took over one horse from Scotch Greys which was destroyed, also destroyed on Col: 2 da. R.H. & one 6th Cav. Fd. Amb. & on 5th M.G. Sqn. Evacuation	
	28th		Thirty-one horses from ESTREES-ST-DENIS & th. & St. Hosp. FORGES-LES-EAUX. Received one twelve cask Amer. from COMPIEGNE & No 7 Vy. Hosp.	
	29th		CHOISY & marched to HIRION.	
HIRION	30th		HIRION & moved to wood near SAINS-EN-AMIENOIS.	

Clement J. L. Ryan.

Vol 39

Confidential
Mun Desp
of
Ma 13 Atabek Adji Reshin

From 1-4-18
To 30-4-18

WAR DIARY
or
INTELLIGENCE SUMMARY
(Erase heading not required.)

Army Form C. 2118.

Instructions regarding War Diaries and Intelligence Summaries are contained in F. S. Regs., Part II. and the Staff Manual respectively. Title pages will be prepared in manuscript.

Place	Date	Hour	Summary of Events and Information	Remarks and references to Appendices
	1.4.18		Moved to BOYES WOOD. O.C. and eight O.R. proceeded to GENTELLES WOOD, and were attached to 1st Cav. Bde. Sent back to Main M.R. 8 eight wounded horses sent on truck of 1st D. 6th and one attached horse of 8th M.G. Sqn. Prototypes are trucks of Y 1st D. 6th e/cR.	
	2nd		O.C. and eight O.R. returned to BOYES wood, and three ration parties to	
BLANGY TRONVILLE			BLANGY-TRONVILLE. c/cR	
FOUILLY.	3rd		Moved to FOUILLOY. c/cR	
	4th		O.C. and five men went as advance party collecting BDE. to near VILLERS BRETONNEUX. Destroyed five horses of 3rd Ivy. Gds. with bad shell wounds and one stray horse with fracture Metatarsalbone. Brought back one wounded horse to FOUILLOY. Received this wounded horse from 1st Canadian c/cR.	
	5th		Evacuated thirty horses through Canadian M & Sect. following units: Hd. Qrs. 6th Cav. Bde, 1 horse, 8th M.G. Sqn, 3rd Sqn. Gds. 9 1st Royals 13, I R Hussars 2, 5th M.G. Bde 1, 1st Lancers 2. Foundings 1 c/cR	
CAMON.	6th		Moved to CAMON. c/cR Clement J O'Ryan Capt.	

WAR DIARY or INTELLIGENCE SUMMARY

Army Form C. 2118.

(Erase heading not required.)

Instructions regarding War Diaries and Intelligence Summaries are contained in F. S. Regs., Part II. and the Staff Manual respectively. Title pages will be prepared in manuscript.

Place	Date	Hour	Summary of Events and Information	Remarks and references to Appendices
CAMON	7/7/18		Took over the following horses for Evacuation: F.R. Hudson 6. 6th O.C. Sqd. 5. 1st Royals 4. 3rd Dragoon Gds. 3. C.I.C.R.	
	8th		Took over one horse from 1st Royals + one from F.R. Hudson. Evacuation.	
			Twenty five B "A" Canadian mobile Vety Section at SALEUX. C.I.C.R.	
	9th		Took over six horses from 3rd Drag. Gds. one from 6th M.G. Sqn. and Evacuation cases to B "A" Canadian mobile Vety Section at SALEUX. C.I.C.R.	
	10th		Took over four horses from 1st K.E.H. 6 Gds. Can from F.R. Hudson. one from 2nd B.Bn. 4 one from "C Batty" R.H.A. Evacuation. B "A" Canadian M.V.S. at BALEUX. C.I.C.R.	
	11th		Left CAMON. went to BUIRE-AUX-BOIS. Evacuation four horses to BALEUX 5/7/18	
BUIRE-AUX-BOIS	12th		Left BUIRE-AUX-BOIS + marched to CONTIVILLE. C.I.C.R.	
CONTIVILLE	13th		Left CONTIVILLE + arrived at BAILLEUL-LES-PERNES. Took over eleven horses from 3rd Drag. Gds. + ten from F.R. Hudson. Left on 9.L. Cav Bde H.Q. orders	
			with the March of BAILLEUL-LES-PERNES. Good off at 2 p.m. + marched to FERFAY. C.I.C.R.	
FERFAY				

Clement C. Ryan Capt.

Reference LENS.14. AMIENS.14. HAZEBROUCK.5.A.) Scale 100,000

WAR DIARY or INTELLIGENCE SUMMARY

Army Form C. 2118.

(Erase heading not required.)

Place	Date	Hour	Summary of Events and Information	Remarks and references to Appendices
FERFAY	14/16		Took over the horses from 1st Squad from from 3rd Troop Gds Goh X R Hussars	
			and 8" Hussars and 5" M.G. Sqd. Brunetta training at NEUCHATEL CHR	
	15:		Took over from horse from 1st Squad Amn from 1st M.G. Sqd. & X R Hussars	
			3 horse mules from 4th Batt R.H.A. Amn Col Brunetta down to NEUCHATEL CHR	
	17:		Took over three horses from 1st Pos R. H.A. ECR	
	18:		Took over two horses from 1st Squad. ECR	
	19:		Took over two horses from A.O.C. Cav Gds Bde 5" Tsp Gds & Men R.R. Hussars	
			Brunetta Man to NEUCHATEL M. F.3.403. Gds WALDER J ASC horses	
			on duty from No. 15 Fld. Hosp. ECR	
	21:		Took our own horse from 1st Regulation from 8th M.G. Sqd. Brunetta	
			eaten horses at NEUCHATEL ECR	
	23:		Took our from horse from 3rd Troop Gds CHR	
FONTAINE LEZ-HERMAN B	24:		Marched from FERFAY to FONTAINE-LEZ-HERMAN B. Took out our own	
			from 3rd Troop Gds ECR	
	25:		Took over five horses from X R Hussars 4 or from 1st M.G. Sqd. CHR	
	29:		Took over one horse from 3rd Lab Battn and 1st Squad Brunetta sitting a NEUCHATEL	
	30:		Took our two mules from 502 G.S.O. and two horses from X R Hussars CHR	

Element J C Ryan Capt.

Confidential

War Diary
of
No. 13 Mobile Vety. Section.

From 1-5-18   To 31-5-18.

Vol 40

WAR DIARY or INTELLIGENCE SUMMARY

Army Form C. 2118.

(Erase heading not required.)

Instructions regarding War Diaries and Intelligence Summaries are contained in F. S. Regs., Part II. and the Staff Manual respectively. Title pages will be prepared in manuscript.

Place	Date	Hour	Summary of Events and Information	Remarks and references to Appendices
FONTAINE-LEZ-HERMANS	9/5/18		Took over two horse for evacuation from 2nd Royal Dragoons. C/ER	
	2/5/18	3pm	Evacuated one horse & two mules to Mo. 13 Sely Hospl. & took over two horses from I.R. Hussars. C/ER	
		4pm	O.C. Sqn. FONTAINE-LEZ-HERMANS & marched to VACQUERIE-LE-BOUCQ. C/ER	
		5pm	O.C. Sqn. VACQUERIE-LE-BOUCQ & marched to FROHEN-LE-GRAND. C/ER	
		6pm	O.C. Sqn. FROHEN-LE-GRAND & marched to CONTAY. C/ER	
CONTAY	7/5	7am	Took over one horse from 2nd Dragoons and two from I.R. Hussars. C/ER	
		8am	Took over four horses from 3rd Dragoons, one from 2nd Dra. Gds, one from the Rob. H. Can. Dra. C/ER	
			Evacuated thirteen horses & one mule to Y.E.8. at OKENCOURT. C/ER	
			CHATEAU. Mo. 33 bill. Driver SMITH J. A.S.C. reported for duty from 4th Co. A.S.C. 3rd Cav. Div. to complete mess. Establishment. C/ER	
		9am	Took over one horse from I.R. Hussars. C/ER	
		10am	Evacuated fourteen horses to Mo. 15. Cely Hospl. Took over the following horses from "C" Batty. R.G.A. Six from 1st Dragds., one MM R 5th Can. Gds. One 6th M.G. Sqn. One "O" Batty. R.H.A. - two from 2 & 2. H.A. Bde. C/ER	

Army Form C. 2118.

WAR DIARY
or
INTELLIGENCE SUMMARY.
(Erase heading not required.)

Instructions regarding War Diaries and Intelligence Summaries are contained in F. S. Regs., Part II. and the Staff Manual respectively. Title pages will be prepared in manuscript.

Place	Date	Hour	Summary of Events and Information	Remarks and references to Appendices
CONTAY	11.5.18		Took over our lines from 282 A.F.A. Bn. C.U.S.	
	12"		Took over our lines from 102 R. Howzers & one from 12th Royals.	
	13"		" Six horses from 3rd Tray. Gds. One from 6th Bde. R.H.A.	
	14"		11th Cdn. Bn from 16th R. Howzers & one from the An. 3rd Cav. Div. C.F.A. Took over one from "C" Batty R.H.A. & Evacuation Hosp.	
			1 No.15. Stj. Hospt. C.C.S.	
	15"		1 S.B.B. unfit sicken & casualties sick animals. Took over one horse from 3rd Tray. Gd. One from 16th R. Howzers. Rd. "C" Batty R.H.A. from 3rd Tray. Gd.	
	16"		Took over one Charger from "C" Batty R.H.A. Rd from 3rd Tray. Gb. & 1 exhib. from 1st Royals	
	17"		Left CONTAY & marched to BELLOY-SUR-SOMME. Evacuated sick horses to No.15. Vety. Hosp. by Ry. frm. PONTAIN-VILLE-MR.	
BELLOY-SUR-SOMME	19"		Took over horse fr T.R. Hooper luces also three Royals & one from 3rd Tray. Gds. C.F.A.	
	20"		Evacuated six sick horses to No.19. V.E.B at PICQUIGNY. Collected a Charger from H.Qrs. 3rd Can. Div. & Evacuated same to No.14 Vety. Hosp by Royal.	

Clement C. Ryan. Capt. A.V.C.(R)

Ref: AMIENS.17
LENS.11

WAR DIARY
or
INTELLIGENCE SUMMARY.

Army Form C. 2118.

Place	Date	Hour	Summary of Events and Information	Remarks and references to Appendices
BELLOY SUR SOMME	22/8		Took over disposition from 5th M.G. Sqn. C/CR	
	23rd		Wire laid from 2nd Bgde. Hrs. to 1st B. Hussars. Lieut B. S. Gibb	
			Reconnaissance sent to 14th. V.E.B. C/CR	
	24th		Wire out on lines from "C" Batty Q.H. to C/CR	
	27th		" " " 3rd Hrs. Sqd. to C/CR	
	28th		" " " "C" Batty Q.H. to " " C/CR	
	29th		fire " "C" Batty Q.H. & H. 3rd S.Gb.	
			Took over from Sd. Sn. 6th Cav. Bde. Line from 1st Bgde. in 3rd S.Gb.	
			On I.R. Advance & evacuation down to Hs. 19 S.S.B. C/CR	
	30th		Returned to line 1 – 2nd Bgde. Cav. took over the new lines from	
			1st Bgde. also line 3rd Dvy. Sqn. Sn. I.R. Hqrs. to "C" Batty R.H.	
	31st		Left BELLOY & marched to MONTIGNY. Took over line side	
			lines which were left in billet by Sq. No 4th M.V.B. C/CR	

Clement J.C. Ryan
Capt. Ave (CSR)

Vol 4

Confidential
War Diary
of
M.B. Mobile Vety Section

From 1-6-16. To 30-6-16.

WAR DIARY or INTELLIGENCE SUMMARY

Army Form C. 2118.

Place	Date	Hour	Summary of Events and Information	Remarks and references to Appendices
MONTIGNY	3-2-18		Took over the following stations for evacuation. 1st Royal Dragoons Van Lorn, 10th R Hussars from "C" Batty R.H.A Rin, 3rd Dg Gds. on e/cR	
	4		Took over from down from 1st M.G. Sqn. Lancashire Battalion to Mo's Rec Stat.	
	5		Took over from horses from 2nd Royals, G.O.C. in charge on Field Ambulance	
	6		Evacuation as with. Horses to M.D.S. Sick took Lost out on from 2nd Brigade	
	7		Evacuation as ustl. Horses to M.D.S. Sick took Lost out on e/cR	
	8		Destroyed one of R.C.H.B. Horses on e/cR	
			Took over on horses from 11th RL Hussars e/cR	
	9		Destroyed one of 3rd Dg Gds. Also 4 took over for other cases from 1st Cav Bde	
	10		Took over the following horses for evacuation. One 1st Royals on e/cR	
			One 13th Hussars Batty R.H.A. e/cR	
	11		Evacuation as usu. horses to Adv. 13th Rec Hosp. e/cR	
	12		Destroyed one of 10th A.R. Hussars. e/cR	
	13		Took over on horses from III Corps Troops e/cR	
	14		1st J/ MONTIGNY + marched to BELLOY-SUR-SOMME e/cR	
BELLOY	15		Took over horses from "C" Batty R.H.A. e/cR	
SUR-SOMME	16		Evacuation for horses to M.D.S.B. e/cR	

Clement J C Ryan

Lafarce AMIENS 17
Scale 100,000

WAR DIARY
or
INTELLIGENCE SUMMARY.

Army Form C. 2118.

Place	Date	Hour	Summary of Events and Information	Remarks and references to Appendices
BELLOY	11/7/18		Took over m. Horses from 1st M.G. Sqn. C/C/R	
	16th		Dismantic or horses by Inspection & M.V.O. 2.8.8. C/CR	
	19th		Took over on loan from 3rd Sup Sqn R.B. C/CR	
	20th		Took over from 1st R. Hussars C/CR	
	21st		Evacuated from h. M.V. 2.8.8. C/CR	
	22nd/23rd		7.D V.B in Company with D.D.V.S. Inspected sickin & suspected sick Horses — C/CR	
			No. 266 Corpl RIBBENS, G. A.C. Dismantled & Evacuated sick Horses — C/CR	
	23rd		Took over on loan from "C" Batty 2nd Sqn 15th M.G.Sqn C/CR	
	24th		Took over on loan from 3rd Royal Van from 3rd Troy S.L. Dismantled	
			one ox 5 No.19 2.8.8. C/CR	
	25th		Took over on loan from 1st Carpoh & one from 3rd Troy Fd. Dismantled 1 Horse of J.8.	
	26th		Took over on loan from 3rd Sup Sqn C/CR	
	27th		Took over on horses from 1st R. Hussars one 3rd L. Horse one 2nd Carpok one 6th M.G. Sqn one	
	29th		Dismantled eight Horses to M.V. 2.8.8. & took over on loan from 3rd Troy F.A. C/CR	

Clement J. C. Ryan

Lefeurre AMIENS.19
100,000
Sick

Confidential

War Diary of
No. 13 Mobile Vety. Section.

From 1.4.18.   To 31.4.18.

WAR DIARY
or
INTELLIGENCE SUMMARY
(Erase heading not required.)

Army Form C. 2118.

Place	Date	Hour	Summary of Events and Information	Remarks and references to Appendices
LE-MESGE	1.7.18		Took over our horses from Lt. Col. 6th Cav. Bde. C/CR	
	2nd		9/E 2,3,4,9. 2/Lt. SKINNER E. admitted to No.41 C.C.S. & struck off strength	
			By Mail. C/CR	
	3rd		Took over the following horses for evacuation 3rd Troop Lt. W. F.R. Hussars one	
			Hd. Qrs. 6th Cav. Bde. one. 1st Royals. two. C/CR	
	4th		Collected a mule from D.A.D.O.S. 3rd Cav. Div. Evacuated eq. Lt. Lewis to No.19 C.C.S.	
	5th, 6th, 7th		Returned one horse to 3rd Sqd. Sgt. 6 duty cases C/CR	
	8th		Ponies. C/CR	
	9th		Took over our horses from Lt. M.G. Sqd. & three from 3rd Troop Lt. C/CR	
	10th		Transferred our mule collection from D.A.D.O.S. to Lt. M.G. Sqd. C/CR	
	12th		Took out our tops from 1st Royals. C/CR	
	13th		Evacuated one horse to No.19 C.C.S. Took one horse from Lt. M.G. Sqd.	
			One from F.R. Hussars. 9/E 28,9,29. 2/Lt. Griffiths L.R.C. rejoins for	
			duty from No. 2 Lt. Hosp. 4 completed rem. establishment. C/CR	
	15th		Took over our horses from 8th Troop Lt. C/CR	
	17th		" " " from 6th Lt. M.G. Sqd.	
			Clement J C Ryan	

Reference HM1EN8.17
8ccb 100,000

WAR DIARY
INTELLIGENCE SUMMARY
(Erase heading not required.)

Army Form C. 2118.

Place	Date	Hour	Summary of Events and Information	Remarks and references to Appendices
LE-MESGE	18th		Took over his horse from 6th M.G. Sqn. on 3rd Stroy fate of mare from I.R. Hudson	C/ER
	19th		S/E 3256. Pte. Seaman W. proceeded on 14 days leave to U.K. C/ER	
	20th		Took over his horse from I.R. Hudson & his from 3rd Stroy fate. C/ER	
	21st		S/E 9344. Corpl. Brown R. of proceeded on his days leave in France.	
			A/H/Corpl. Skellin A. proceeded on a seven days Gas course at the Cav. Corps Gas School C/ER	
	22nd		A.D.V.S. inspected the section 6/ER	
	24th		Evacuated four horses to No. 19. V.S.S. C/ER	
	27th		Took over six horses from I.R. Hudson & his from 1st Royal C/ER	
	28th		Took over his horse from 1st Royals 4 December Horses to No. 19 V.S.S.	
	29th		No. 653. Pte Macdonald. J. reported for duty from No. 2 Sep. Hospital	

Clement C Ryan

CONFIDENTIAL

War Diary of
No. 13. Mobile Vety. Section.
From 1-8-18.   To 31-8-18.

Army Form C. 2118.

WAR DIARY
or
INTELLIGENCE SUMMARY.

Reforma
AMIENS. 1/9.
Scale 1/100,000.

(Erase heading not required.)

Place	Date	Hour	Summary of Events and Information	Remarks and references to Appendices
LE-MESGE	8/18		Routine	
	2nd		Took over two sick horses from 10th R. Hussars & one from 3rd Gen. Evacuating the horses to No.19 V.S. & C.P.R.	
	3rd		Took over two horses from 6th M.G. Sqdn. & one from 1st R. Royals. One 10th R. Hussars. On 3rd G. Gn. & evacuated same to No. 19 V.S. & C.P.R.	
	6th		Left LE-MESGE & marched with Brigade to RENANCOURT. C.P.R.	
RENANCOURT	7th		Posted a Sergt. & three men with 9th & 2nd Royal Dragoons. Took over two horses from 10th R. Hussars & one from 4th A.H. on 6th Cav. Bde. Left RENANCOURT at 6 A.M. & marched under orders of A.D.V.S. 3rd Cav. Div. to SALEUX. Seen then with a Rear Canadian M.V.S. & but from 14th M.V.S. C.P.R.	
SALEUX	8th		Evacuated two O.R. with four horses from 10th R. Hussars C.P.R.	
	9th		Evacuated two horses through the 4th Canadian M.V.S. which was acting as a V.S.B. at SALEUX. D.D.V.S. 4th Army invited for inspection. Took over twenty nine sick animals from No.10 M.V.S. & four from No.7 M.V.S. & fifty three from No.14th M.V.S. C.P.R.	

Clement J. C. Byrne

Army Form C. 2118.

WAR DIARY
or
INTELLIGENCE SUMMARY.
(Erase heading not required.)

Reference AMIENS 1 Y.
Feat 1/40,000.

Instructions regarding War Diaries and Intelligence Summaries are contained in F. S. Regs., Part II. and the Staff Manual respectively. Title pages will be prepared in manuscript.

Place	Date	Hour	Summary of Events and Information	Remarks and references to Appendices
SALEUX	9/8		Received one horse cart by O.D.R. 3rd Army & fourteen sick animals of various units. Sent seven O.R's, which had been sent down with horse, to Cav: Corps: Reinforcement Camp. ABBEVILLE. Proceed to BOYES.	
	10th		Relieved No. 14 M.V.S. under orders of A.D.V.S. 3rd Cav. Div. Handed over one hundred & eight sick animals to V.E.S. after being SALEUX. c/cR	
	11th		Received one hundred & four animals from No.14 M.V.S. & evacuated same to V.E.S. at SALEUX. c/cR	
	12th		Received forty-eight animals from No.14 M.V.S. & evacuated eleven to V.S.S. at SALEUX. c/cR	
	13th		Received ninety-two sick animals from 14 M.V.S. & evacuated thirty-six to V.S.S. SALEUX & sent fifty-three to the Canadian Corps V.S.S. at BOVES. c/cR	
FOUENCAMPS	13th 14th		Received four sick horses from 8th M.G.B. & moved from BOVES to FOUENCAMPS. eight " " from 1st Royals. third from 3rd Army Gds. & Evacuated twelve to the Canadian Mobile V.S.S. at BOVES. c/cR	
	15th		Received three horses from 3rd Army Gds. One from 1st Royals & one All Or. S. Ca Bds. Evacuated same to Can. V.S.P. Marched from FOUENCAMPS to MESGE. c/cR
Lieut J.C. Ryan	

WAR DIARY or INTELLIGENCE SUMMARY.

Army Form C. 2118.

Reference AMIENS. 1/4
Scale 1/100,000
LENS. 11. 1/100,000

Instructions regarding War Diaries and Intelligence Summaries are contained in F. S. Regs., Part II. and the Staff Manual respectively. Title pages will be prepared in manuscript.

Place	Date	Hour	Summary of Events and Information	Remarks and references to Appendices
LE-MESGE	16/8/18		Routine. C/CR	
	17"		Received three sick horses from 16th R. Hussars & one from 13th Royals. C/CR	
	18"		Routine. C/CR	
	19"		Received two horses from 3rd L. Gds. & one remount from 6th No. 19. A.B.S. C/CR	
	20"		" " 10th R. Hussars. Also H.A.C.? Cav. Bde. & one 6th C.T.R. C/CR	
	21"		Moved from LE-MESGE at 12.5 p.m. & marched to FIEFFES. Left all sick animals with "B" Sectn. C/CR	
FIEFFES	22"		Took over our sick horse from 6th M.G. Sqn. C/CR	
	23"		" " " " 6th M.G.S. C/CR	
	25"		Left FIEFFES at 10 p.m. & marched to GUESCHART. arriving at 3.50 a.m. C/CR	
	26"		Left GUESCHART & marched to NUNCQ. C/CR	
NUNCQ	27"		Took over one horse from 10th R. Hussars. Four 6th M.G. Sqn & one H.Q. & 6th Co. Rfl. C/CR	
	28"		" " 1st Royals. One from 10th R. Hussars & two 3rd L. Gds.	
	29"		Evacuated eleven to dep. Collecting Stn. at ST. POL. C/CR	
	29"		Evacuated twelve sick animals to A.C.P. ST-POL & received three from 10th R. Hussars. One from 1st Royals & one from 3rd L. Gds. C/CR	
			Almert J.C.Ryan	

Confidential

War Diary

No. 13. Mobile Lab Section

From 1: 9: 18.   to 30: 9: 18.

Army Form C. 2118.

WAR DIARY
of
INTELLIGENCE SUMMARY.
(Erase heading not required.)

Place	Date	Hour	Summary of Events and Information	Remarks and references to Appendices
NUNCQ	1/18		D.D.V.S. visited the section. Took over a sick horse from I.R. Huzzar. E/CR	
	2nd		Received the following animals for evacuation 2.3rd S.Gds. 1.I.R. Huzzar. 2.5th M.G.Sqn. 1. Mule from Reserve Park 3rd Cav. Div. e/CCR	
			Took over 2 horses from 3rd Dragoon Gds. + 1 from 1st + 2nd Royals. e/CCR	
	3rd		" " C" Batty. R.H.A. 1 from 5th Cav. Fd. Ambl. + 4 from 1st + 2nd Royals	
	4th		Evacuated 16 horses + 1 mule to Vety Collecting Sol. ST.POL. 2/CR	
	6th		Left NUNCQ + marched with the Brigade to LE-PLACITON. 2/CR	
	7th		Received four horses from I.R. Huzzar. Capt. c/c C. RYAN. A.V.C. proceeded on leave to U.K.	
	8th		" " one horse from 1.3rd R. Dragoons + 1 from 3rd Fd. Sqn R.E.	
	9th		Evacuated 10 sick horses to No.13. Vety Hospl. + took over 3 from	
			"C" Batty R.H.A. + 1. from 1st + 2nd Royals e/CR	
			Took over one mule from 3rd Cav Div. Res. Pk. e/CR	
	13th		" " two horses from I.R. Huzzar. e/CR	
	15th		" " one horse from R.C.H.A. + evacuated 4 to No.13. Vety Hospl.	
	16th		One Sergt + nine men joined the Batn. to take part in Tactical Exercises	
			Carried out. by the 3rd Cav. Div. e/CR	
			Clement JC Ryan Capt.	

B/LENS II

WAR DIARY
or
INTELLIGENCE SUMMARY.
(Erase heading not required.)

Army Form C. 2118.

Instructions regarding War Diaries and Intelligence Summaries are contained in F. S. Regs., Part II. and the Staff Manual respectively. Title pages will be prepared in manuscript.

Place	Date	Hour	Summary of Events and Information	Remarks and references to Appendices
LE-PLACITON	1918		Left LE-PLACITON & marched with Brigade to REBREUVE e/cR	
	20th		Admitted 2 sick from 1st Dr. Royals. & from I.R. Hussars. & 1. 6th Sig. Troop	
	22nd		Capt. E. J. E. RYAN. A.V.C. returning from leave. e/cR	
	23rd		Evacuated 4 horses to No. 14. Vety. Hospl. & took over 1 from I.R. Hussars & 1. 3rd Dr. Gds. e/cR	
	25th		Marched from REBREUVE to BUS-LES-ARTOIS. Took over 3 horses from 1. 2nd Royals. & 1. I.R. Hussars to 2.6th M.G. Sqn. Evacuated 12 horses to No. 14. Vety. Hospl. e/cR	
	26th		Left BUS-LES-ARTOIS & marched to a point about 1 Km south of ALBERT. Took over to sick horses of 3rd Dr. Inns. Gds. e/cR	
	27th		Marched to H.E.M. Took over 4 sick horses of I.R. Hussars & 1 Mule B. Cav. Corps Res. Pk. e/cR	
	29th		Took over 3 horses of 3rd Dr. Gds. 4. 1. Dr. Royals. & 1. from 1st C.F.S. Evacuated 17. horses to No. 3. Vety. Evacuation Section. Marched with the Bde to VERMAND. e/cRyan	

Clements J. C. Ryan Capt.

WAR DIARY
or
INTELLIGENCE SUMMARY.
(Erase heading not required.)

Army Form C. 2118.

Place	Date	Hour	Summary of Events and Information	Remarks and references to Appendices
VERMAND	30/10		Took over pive sick horses from 6th M.G. Sqn. one horse from 6th Bde. R.H.A. one hr. 4 6th Bn 2 Bty R.H.A. one hr. and one from 3rd Sqd L.G. C.G.R. cleaned dispersed	

Clement JC Ryan Capt.

Re/ ST QUENTIN 18

CONFIDENTIAL.

WAR DIARY

OF

No. 13 MOBILE VETERINARY SECTION.

FROM 1:10:18.   TO 31:10:18.

Army Form C. 2118.

WAR DIARY
or
INTELLIGENCE SUMMARY.
Reference
ST. QUENTIN. 18.
100,000
(Erase heading not required.)

Instructions regarding War Diaries and Intelligence Summaries are contained in F. S. Regs., Vol. II. and the Staff Manual respectively. Title pages will be prepared in manuscript.

Place	Date	Hour	Summary of Events and Information	Remarks and references to Appendices
VERMAND	1/10/18		Evacuation 18 horse to "A" Canadian Mobil Vety Section. CJCR	
	2nd		Troops from VERMAND to near BELLENGLISE, return on present motorlive	
			from A.D.V.S. 3rd Can. Div. to return to VERMAND. Took over 4 sick	
			horse & evacuation to "A" Canadian M.V.S. CJCR	
	3rd		Took over 4 horse & evacuation 9 to "A" Can. M.V.S. Moved from	
			VERMAND to BELLENGLISE. CJCR	
	4th		Took over 22 sick animals. Evacuation 21 to "A" Can. M.V.S. CJCR	
	5th		Took over 13 sick horse & mules to YPRES-CON CJCR	
FREFCON.	6th		A.D.V.S. in Company with D.D.V.S. visited the section. Evacuation 13	
			horse to "A" Can. M.V.S. CJCR	
	7th		Left TREFCON & marched to BELLENGLISE. Received 16 sick horse	
			& evacuation 14 to "A" Can. M.V.S. CJCR	
	8th		Left BELLENGLISE & went to ESTREES, when we received	
			orders from A.D.V.S. to remain there the day & return to the	
			same Billets at BELLENGLISE at night. CJCR	
	9th		Returned to the same place near ESTREES at 6.30 A.M. CJCR	
			Clement J C Ryan	

WAR DIARY

Reference VALENCIENNES 12   SHEET 57.Y.C   ST. QUENTIN 78

INTELLIGENCE SUMMARY

Army Form C. 2118.

Scale 1/40,000   1/40,000   1/100,000

Instructions regarding War Diaries and Intelligence Summaries are contained in F.S. Regs., Part II. and the Staff Manual respectively. Title pages will be prepared in manuscript.

(Erase heading not required.)

Place	Date	Hour	Summary of Events and Information	Remarks and references to Appendices
ESTRÉES.	9/10/18.		Moved to GENEVE & thence to area MARETZ, wounded and received 14. sick and wounded horses & evacuated same to No. 54. M.V.S. Moved into BIERAIN farm at night & received 51 sick animals from 14th M.V.S. C/CC	
SERAIN FARM.	10th		Evacuated 112 horses to "A" Canadian M.V.S. C/CC	
	11th		Received 40 horses from 14 5th M.V.S. 43 of which we evacuated to "A" Can. M.V.S. C/CC	
	12th		Received 16 horses from 14th M.V.S. & evacuated them to "A" Can M.V.S. Visited "A" Can. M.V.S. at GENEVE to help to evacuate the sick horses that had been collected they about 350 in number. C/CC	
	13th		Having closed GENEVE of sick horses opened S. Can. Pits at BANTUEX. C/CC	
	14th		Took over of sick horses from the T.R. Hazers & Quentin Horrel No. T.E.B. Moved to HENOIS wood C/CC	
HENOIS WOOD.	15th		Took over 25 sick horses C/CC	
	16th		Evacuated 26 horses from Mo. 4. V.E.S. C/CC	
	18th		Took over 20 sick horses C/CC	
	19th		Evacuated 20 horses to No. 13. V.E.S. C/CC	

Clement J C Ryan

Army Form C. 2118.

WAR DIARY
or
INTELLIGENCE SUMMARY.

(Erase heading not required.)

Reforme 8 deel 5 Y.C. / 40,000

Instructions regarding War Diaries and Intelligence Summaries are contained in F. S. Regs., Part II. and the Staff Manual respectively. Title pages will be prepared in manuscript.

Place	Date	Hour	Summary of Events and Information	Remarks and references to Appendices
HENOIS WOOD	21/10/18		Received 12 sick horses + evacuated same to No. 13 V.E.S. CCR	
	23"		Received 2 sick horses. CCR	
	24"		" " " " CCR	
	25"		Evacuated 11 horses to No. 2 American V.E.S. CCR	
	27"		Took over 19 horses CCR	
	29"		Evacuated 19 " to No. 1 Vety Hospl. CCR	
	30"		Took over 10 horses for evacuation. CCR	

Clement F. O'Ryan

Confidential

War Diary
of
No. 13. Mobile Vet Section.

From 1.11.18.
To 30.11.18.

WAR DIARY or INTELLIGENCE SUMMARY

Army Form C. 2118.

Place	Date	Hour	Summary of Events and Information	Remarks and references to Appendices
HENNOIS WOOD	1/18		Took over four sick horses & evacuated fourteen to No. 4 Vety. Hospl. EFCR	
MANANCOURT	3rd		Took over seven sick horses. EFCR	
	4th		" " six " " " EFCR	
	5th		Evacuated thirteen horses to No. 4 Vety. Hospl. EFCR	
	6th		Left HENNOIS-WOOD & marched to MARQUION. EFCR	
	7th		Marched to ESQUERCHIN. EFCR	
	8th		Marched to PERONNE. Evacuated 200 horses to Mo. 18 Y.E.8. EFCR	
	10th		Received seventeen sick horses & evacuated them to No. 1 Y.E.8. at	
			TEMPLEUVE. Left PERONNE & marched to GAURAIN-RAMECROIX. EFCR	
	11th		Marched to LEUZE & returned to GAURAIN-RAMECROIX at night. EFCR	
	12th		Marched to PONTENCHE. EFCR	
	13th		Attached Brigade Cyclists	
	14th		Attached R.O.Y.8. Regiment at RATOING.	
	15th		Evacuated fifty four sick horses & one mule to No. 3 Y.E.8. at TOURNAI. EFCR	

Clement J. Cooper.

WAR DIARY
or
INTELLIGENCE SUMMARY.
(Erase heading not required.)

Army Form C. 2118.

Instructions regarding War Diaries and Intelligence Summaries are contained in F. S. Regs., Part II. and the Staff Manual respectively. Title pages will be prepared in manuscript.

Place	Date	Hour	Summary of Events and Information	Remarks and references to Appendices
PONTENCHE	15th		Evacuated chown sick hors & one mule b/ No.3. Y.E.S. at TOURNAI. e/cR	
	17th		Left PONTENCHE & marched to CROISETTE. e/cR	
	18th		marched to SAINTES. e/cR	
	19th		Took on fifteen sick horses e/cR	
	20th		Evacuated fifteen to 'A' Canadian M.V.S. who had formed a Collecting Post near GAMMONT. e/cR	
	21st		moved to OTTIGNIES e/cR	
	22nd		moved to EGHEZEE. (Via WATERLOO) e/cR	
	24th		moved to UPIGNY. e/cR	
	25th		Took on thirteen sick horses e/cR	
	26th		" " ten " e/cR	
	29th		" " two " e/cR	

Clement J C Ryan

Reference TOURNAI 5 - 100,000
BRUSSELS 6 - 100,000

Confidential

Alex Geary
of
No. 13 Frederick Ictz Sector

From 1-12-18   To 31-12-18

Army Form C. 2118.

WAR DIARY
or
INTELLIGENCE SUMMARY.
(Erase heading not required.)

Instructions regarding War Diaries and Intelligence Summaries are contained in F. S. Regs., Part II. and the Staff Manual respectively. Title pages will be prepared in manuscript.

Place	Date	Hour	Summary of Events and Information	Remarks and references to Appendices
UPIGNY	3/8/14		A D.M.S 3rd Cavalry Division visited the unit. *ECCR*	
	4.		Received 19 Horses + 1 mule from "A" Canadian M/S – 4 came from 14th V.S. *ECCR*	
	5		Evacuated 27 Horses + one mule to the 2 V.E.S NAMUR *ECCR*	
	8		Received 3 horses from 6th h.g. Sqd. Then 3 Op. 2 I R Hussars + one from 1st Royal Dragoons. *ECCR*	
	9		Evacuated 13 Horses to Canadian V.E.S at NAMUR *ECCR*	
	10		Moved from UPIGNY to VINACHMONT *ECCR*	
	12		moved to STO MAY *ECCR*	
	20.		Received one Horse from 3 D my Guards. *ECCR*	
	23		Received one horse from 2 R Hussars + one from "C" Batty R.H.A. *ECCR*	
	28		Received 4 horses from 1st Royal Dragoons + 2 "E" Batty R.H.A	
	29		Received 8 horses from 1st Royal Dragoons. 1 from H.L. "C" Sqn Pole + one from 6th h.L. Sqd.	
	30		Evacuated 17 horses to 20,13 Vety Hospital at WELLCHATEL from ENG.15 Rentlered *ECCR* Elmout J. C. Ryan	

Reference BRUSSELS 100,000
LIEGE 100,000

CONFIDENTIAL.

WAR DIARY.

13 M V S

January 1919.

WAR DIARY or INTELLIGENCE SUMMARY

Army Form C. 2118.

Place	Date	Hour	Summary of Events and Information	Remarks and references to Appendices
STOCKAY St GEORGE	1-1-19		Receive 2 Horses from C/O May. R.H.A. & one from 3rd Royal Dragoons C/CR	
	2-1-19		Receive 1 Horse from 10th Royal Hussars C/CR	
	6-1-19		Received 1 Charger from 1st Royal Dragoons C/CR	
LIEGE 1/100,000	7-1-19		Received 2 Horses from 1st Royal Dragoons & 1 Horse from 6th M. Reserve Gun Spl. Red	
	9-1-19		Received 2 Horses from G radiation & Horse 10 ly Hussars & 1 Charger 1st Royal Dragoons Red	
	10-1-19		Received 4 Horses & one Mule from 3rd Royal Dragoons Gas C/CR	
	12-1-19		Received 3 Horses & one Mule from 3rd Royal Dragoons & 2 from 3rd Dragoons Gas C/CR	
	13-1-19		Received 2 Mules from 1st Royal Dragoons C/CR	
	16-1-19		Received 2 Mules & Horse C/Battery R.H.A. 14, 1st Royal Dragoons 13, 10th Royal Hussars	
	20-1-19		Received 3 Mules C/Battery R.H.A. & 33rd Hussars Gds & 1, 3rd Dragoon Gds	
	21-1-19		H.Q. Veterinary Gun Base. 3, 33rd Hussars Gds & 1, 3rd Dragoon Gds. Evacuated 107 Horses & 3 Mules	
			Received 4 Horses & 2 Mules from 14 Fy. M.S.	
			To Advanced Veterinary Hospital C/CR	
	22-1-19		Received 2 Horses from G.W.C. C/CR	
	23-1-19		Received 1 in 1st Royal Dragoons & 1st Battery 7, 3rd Royal Dragoons & 1st Dragoon Gds 6.13 - 7 H.M. Red	
	24-1-19		Received 1 Horse, 1st Royal Dragoons C/CR	
	25-1-19		Received 1 in Royal Dragoons. 2, 6 M.C. Spl. 3, 3rd Horse Gas & 1, Field Ambulance C/CR	
	27-1-19		Received 1 Mare & 1 M.G. Spl. 1, 3rd Royal Dragoons C/CR	
			Received 12 Horses 3rd Pack Gds C/CR	
	28-1-19		Received 1 Horse H.Q. 3rd Dragoon Gds C/CR	
	31-1-19		Received 3 Horses, 1st Royal Dragoons, 6 Horses & 2 Mules from 3rd Dragoon Gds C/CR	
	22-1-19		The above Horses were inspected by A.D.V.S. 3rd Cav. Division & Crossland C/CR	

Clement J. C. Ryan

WAR DIARY or INTELLIGENCE SUMMARY

Army Form C. 2118.

13th Mobile Veterinary Section

Vol 50

February 1919

Place	Date	Hour	Summary of Events and Information	Remarks and references to Appendices
Strazeele St George	1st		Received 7 Horses from 1st Royal Dragoons /1702	
	3rd		" 4 Do from 1st Royal Dragoons /1702	
	5th		Received 2 Horses from 10th Royal Hussars /1702	
	4th		Received 1 Horse from 3rd Dragoon Guards & 3 Horses from 10th Royal Hussars /1702	
	6th		Received 9 Horses from 1st Royal Dragoons /1702	
	8th		Received 3 Horses from 1st Royal Dragoons /1702	
	9th		Received 26 Horses from 6th M.G.Sqdn, 1st Brigade, 4th B.R.B. H.Q Scouts	
	9th		Returned 3 Horses from 1st Royal Dragoons 2 Horses from 10th R. Hussars, 7.6 Thirteenth, 3 Dragoon Gds	
	9th		Evacuated 156 Horses to 2 Field & Advanced Vety Hospital Charleroi /1702	
	11th		Received 2 Horses from 1st Royal Dragoons /1702	
	13th		Received 4 Horses from 1st Royal Dragoons, 1 Horse from 6th M.G.Sqdn /1702	
	14th		Received 1 Horse from 1st Royal Dragoons, 7 Destroyed, 1 Horse 13 Mobile Vety Sec.	
	16th		Received 1 Horse from 3rd Dragoon Guards /1702	
	17th		Received 1 Horse from 7 Royal Dragoons, 1 Horse from 10th R. Hussars /1702	
	18th		Received 1 Horse from 6th B.H.H.Qrs, 2 Horses 13th M. V. Sec., 2 Horses 3rd Dragoon Gds, 2 Horses 1 Tank 7 Brigade	
	18th		Evacuated 18 Horses & one Mule to Advanced Vety Hospital Charleroi /1702	
	19th		Received 12 Horses from Corner Station Cavalry Corps, 1 Horse Cabty R.H.A. 1 Horse 1st R. Dragoons	
	14th		Received 2 Horses on Destruction from 14th M.V.Sec. /119	
	22nd		Received 3 Horses from 1st R. Dragoons, 1 Horse from 10th R. Hussars /1702	
	24th		Received 2 Horses from 1st R. Dragoons /119	
	27th		Received 1 Horse from 10th R. Hussars /119	
	28th		Received 1 Horse from 7 Horse Essex Railway & 1 Horse from E. Battery R.H.A /119	

Clement J. C. Ryan Capt.

WAR DIARY
INTELLIGENCE SUMMARY

Army Form C. 2118.

13th Mobile Veterinary Section Vol 5

March 1919

Place	Date	Hour	Summary of Events and Information	Remarks and references to Appendices
Amal	1st March		Received 3 Horses from 1st R. Dragoons. 2 Horses from Corps Camp Engrs. 1 Horse C. Bty. R.H.A.	
"	2nd "		" 7 " 6th " G. Sqn. 1 " " 3rd Dragoon Guards.	
"	4th "		" 7 " C. Battery R.H.A. RETURNED 2 Horses to 1st Hussars	
"	5th "		" 1 " 2 Horse Camp Shoeing. 1 Mule " 3rd Cav. Bw. A.H.T. 2 Horses from 1st R. Dragoons	
"	6th "		" 1 " 1st R. Dragoons	
"	7th "		" 3 " 3rd Dragoon Guards	
"	8th "		" 3 " 10th Royal Hussars	
"	9th "		" 1 " 6th G. Sqn.	
"	10th "		" 3 " C. Bty. R.H.A. 1 Horse 6th M.G. Sqn. 1 Mule 1st R. Dragoons 2 Mules from 3rd Cav. Bde. A.H.T.	
"	11th "		" 1 " 1st R. Dragoons 1 " 6th Cav. Bde H.Q. 24 Horses from 2 Horse Depot Shoeing Evacuated 3 Horses + 7 Mules	
"	"		" 3rd Cav. Bw. H. Qrs. 1 Concentration Camp Engrs. 1 Horse 3rd Cav. Bde A.H.T. 6 A.V.H. Ghelavi	
"	12th "		" Concentration Camp Engrs	
"	"		" 1st R. Dragoons Section moved from Sickeny to Amay for Bathing	
"	20th "		" Concentration Camp Engrs	
"	21st "		" 1 Mule 3rd Cav Bw. A.H.T.	
"	22nd "		" Concentration Camp Engrs	
"	23rd "		" Do Do	
"	28th "		" 1 Mule 3rd Cav. Bde A.H.T.	
"	30th "		" 2 Horses Concentration Camp Engrs. 2 Horses from Cav Corps Bridging Park.	
"	31st		Evacuated 30 Horses + 2 Mules to A.V. Hospl. DUREN.	

Routine Work

J. Miée Ross
Capt R.A.V.C.
O.C. 13th Mob. Vet. Sect.

Volume 162 April 13 1919 WAR DIARY
D 13414th Bn Middlesex Regiment
INTELLIGENCE SUMMARY
Army Form C.2118.

Place	Date	Hour	Summary of Events and Information	Remarks and references to Appendices
AMAY	1st		Routine work. incidents small	
	2nd		Routine work. nothing of interest	
	3rd		Inspected horses at Calais by Camp ENG.15 for dispatch to base	
	4th		Had show of 144 MGS who to report for course to Calais	
	5th		Routine work. weekly returns and Eff. monthly demand	
	6th		Accounts for Jan & Feb to Brussels dispatched	
			Routine work	
	7th		Inspection 368 horses at annual G.O.C. Inspection dispatched to base	
	8th		Arranged for the despatch of release personnel otherwise 91777 L/C M.P.S. Complete to Cadel to H.Q. W.R. Hospital Valas	
	9th		Released ethnically dispatches to the Quer Troop Calais	
			Inspected horses	
	10th		Released to HAMUR (n° 17721 Mr. H Murray) who was prasted for to England on 13th Feb & failed to return	
	11th		Remanded Pte H Cartwright and instated 2nd Lunnay Officer to W Ahm	

(2)
Volume 163   13th to 14th   Army Form C. 2118.

WAR DIARY or INTELLIGENCE SUMMARY

April   Mobile Vety Section

(Erase heading not required.)

Place	Date	Hour	Summary of Events and Information	Remarks and references to Appendices
AMAY	12th		Routine work, mounted units	
"	13th		The Belgian Au. section 2nd Regt 30 Men 2 Offs 3 S.C.M. attached. Horses of 14th M.V.S. very bad	
"	14th		Completed indent for defences of horses of 14th M.V.S. Vented work	
"	15th		Routine work	
"	16th		" work	
"	17th		Routine work	
"	18th		Received orders to demobilize Sept. to cse Rages	
"	19th		Inspected horses & animals belonging to G.H.Q. ENGIS	
"	20th		Routine work	
"	21st		Sept. to cse horses cleared for demobilize. Routine work	
"	22nd		Routine work	
ENGIS	23rd		Cadre off 13th & 14th M.V.S. move to ENGIS	
AMAY	23rd		Also Villages of Flemalle to 39th Yard Vety tent 1st Div from 14th M.V.S. very left	

(3) Volume 104

1344 † 14 U
Mr V. ty Cohen

WAR DIARY
or
INTELLIGENCE SUMMARY.
(Erase heading not required.)

Army Form C. 2118.

Chol

Instructions regarding War Diaries and Intelligence Summaries are contained in F. S. Regs., Part II. and the Staff Manual respectively. Title pages will be prepared in manuscript.

Place	Date	Hour	Summary of Events and Information	Remarks and references to Appendices
ENGIS	Dec 25th		Sergt Joyce 12th Inn also 13th MS & Pte Hollings ?	
"	26th		10th Cdn Div to duty	
"	27		Routine work	
"	28		" "	
"	29		" "	
"	31		" "	

J Mill
Capt R.A.M.C.
O.C. 13 † † 14 U. 21 Mot Very Lebn.

www.ingramcontent.com/pod-product-compliance
Lightning Source LLC
Chambersburg PA
CBHW081352160426
43192CB00013B/2391